THE BRIDGESTONE
100 BEST PLACES TO STAY IN IRELAND 2004

G000075589

THE BRIDGESTONE

100 BEST
PLACES TO STAY
IN IRELAND 2004

JOHN McKENNA - SALLY McKENNA

ESTRAGON PRESS

FIRST PUBLISHED IN 2004

BY ESTRAGON PRESS

DURRUS

COUNTY CORK

© ESTRAGON PRESS

TEXT © JOHN & SALLY McKENNA

THE MORAL RIGHT OF THE AUTHORS HAS

BEEN ASSERTED

ISBN 1 874076 51 0

PRINTED IN SPAIN BY GRAPHYCEMS

WRITTEN BY JOHN McKENNA

CONTRIBUTING EDITORS:

ORLA BRODERICK

ELIZABETH FIELD

CLAIRE GOODWILLIE

CAROLINE WORKMAN

PUBLISHING EDITOR: SALLY McKENNA

EDITOR: JUDITH CASEY

ART DIRECTION BY NICK CANN

COVER PHOTOS BY MIKE O'TOOLE

ILLUSTRATIONS BY AOIFE WASSER

WEB: FLUIDEDGE.IE

WEB CONTRIBUTING EDITOR: LESLIE WILLIAMS

FOR

HUGH STANCLIFFE

WITH THANKS TO

Colm Conyngham, Des Collins

Frieda Forde, Josette Cadoret,

Margie Deverell, Lelia McKenna,

Mike O'Toole, Ann Marie Tobin,

Miguel Sancho

BRIDGESTONE TYRES

Bridgestone is the world's largest tyre and rubber company.

■ Founded in Japan in 1931, it currently employs over 100,000 people in Europe, Asia and America and its products are sold in more than 150 countries. Its European plants are situated in France, Spain, Italy, Poland and Turkey.

■ Bridgestone manufacture tyres for a wide variety of vehicles from passenger cars and motorcycles, trucks and buses to giant earthmovers and aircraft.

■ Many new cars are fitted with Bridgestone tyres during manufacture including Ford, Toyota, Volkswagen, Mercedes and BMW. Ferrari and Porsche are also fitted with Bridgestone performance tyres as original equipment.

■ Bridgestone commercial vehicle tyres enjoy a worldwide reputation for durability and its aircraft tyres are used by more than 100 airlines.

■ In Formula 1 Bridgestone supply tyres to leading teams and drivers, including Ferrari and Michael Schumacher. Technology developed in the sport has led to increased performance and safety in Bridgestone's road tyres.

■ Bridgestone tyres are distributed in Ireland by Bridgestone Ireland Ltd, a subsidiary of the multinational Bridgestone Corporation. A wide range of tyres is stocked in its 70,000 square foot central warehouse and its staff provide sales, technical and delivery services all over Ireland.

■ Bridgestone tyres are available from First Stop Tyre Centres and tyre dealers throughout Ireland.

FOR FURTHER INFORMATION:

BRIDGESTONE IRELAND LTD
10 Fingal Bay Business Park
Balbriggan
County Dublin
Tel: (01) 841 0000
Fax: (01) 841 5245

34 Hillsborough Road
Lisburn
BT28 1AQ
Tel: (028) 926 78331

websites:
www.bridgestone-eu.com
www.firststop-eu.com

• The Borderlands are coming! After the success of West Waterford in recent years in establishing a critical mass of good addresses, we suddenly have discovered a group of exciting places to eat and stay in the border regions.

• From County Louth through to the border zone of County Donegal, the region now has some truly excellent addresses. So, it's time to celebrate the new places, and time also to praise those who have toiled away here for years, during a time when the region was seen not just as an area devoid of good places, but when it was effectively a no-go area.

• The new addresses also offer excellent value for money, something we have sought with a particular vengeance this year. For it seems to us that many of the country houses in Ireland now offer poor value for money: if you want to find 'rip-off Ireland' you need only stay at some of those grand houses where they will charge hotel prices for domestic cooking and also expect you to pay a healthy tithe to stay in a room just because the house is ancient.

• These people need to wake up: price sensitivity is the new addiction, and those addresses offering value have had another triumphant year in 2003. In the Borderlands. they have realised this, and we reckon their time is now.

John & Sally McKenna
Durrus, West Cork, October 2003

'Their private esperanto is compounded of jazz, horse-racing and malt whiskey.'

– Biographical note on Richard Cook and Brian Morton, 'The Penguin Guide to Jazz'

• Through a dozen years of Bridgestone 100 Best Guides, a pair of enormous, witty, engrossing volumes have sustained us and guided us, enlivened and enlightened us to the possibilities – and the pitfalls – of making repeated judgements on works of art.

• The volumes are 'A Biographical Dictionary of Film' by David Thomson, the fourth edition of which appeared in 2002, and 'The Penguin Guide to Jazz on CD', by Richard Cook and Brian Morton, whose sixth capacious edition appeared in 2002 also.

• For years, we have pored over these books, reading them, re-reading them, arguing with them, finding space in the house to store them – the six Penguin Guides require a decent-sized shelf all to themselves. Thomson and Cook and Morton have sent us rushing to the screen and the CD players, keen to see and hear their discoveries.

an icon

a classic

worth a detour

a comfort zone

• Reading this might make a lot of readers say, 'Aha, so that's where the obscure references to movies and music come from', and others will say, 'So that's why those guys are such a bunch of anoraks! Too many dictionaries!' And that would be partly correct: books like these don't create an obsessive nature, but they sure do feed it.

• But what this trio of critics has taught us, above all, is the necessity, in criticism, to be able to change your mind, and the necessity to write with the strong possibility that you are wrong, and that another opinion can be equally valid. They have shown us that judgements cannot stand still, and that critics and criticism must live and breath and develop. Above all, criticism must be human: the day you write your verdict on tablets of stone, go retire.

• So thank you, David, Richard and Brian. Keep it up, guys.

icons

Assolas Country House, Kanturk

Ballymaloe House, Shanagarry

Buggy's Glencairn Inn, Glencairn

The Clarence, Dublin

Fortview House, Goleen

Kelly's Resort Hotel, Rosslare

Longueville House, Mallow

The Mustard Seed, Echo Lodge, Ballingarry

Newport House, Newport

Norman Villa, Galway

The Quay House, Clifden

Richmond House, Cappoquin

Salville House, Enniscorthy

Shelburne Lodge, Kenmare

Temple House, Ballymote

classic

Ballynahinch Castle, Recess

Ballyvolane House, Fermoy

Blindgate House, Kinsale

Glenally House, Youghal

Iskeroon, Caherdaniel

Kilgraney Country House, Bagenalstown

Killarney Park Hotel, Killarney

The Moat Inn, Templepatrick

The Morrison, Dublin

The Park Hotel, Kenmare

Zuni, Kilkenny

detour

Clifden House, Corofin

Coast Townhouse, Tramore

Dolphin Beach, Clifden

Ghan House, Carlingford

Hilton Park, Clones

Marble Hall, Dublin

Sea Mist, Clifden

Sheen Falls Lodge, Kenmare

comfort zone

Ballyknocken House, Ashford

Beech Hill Country House, Craigantlet

Bow Hall, Castletownshend

Carrig House, Ring of Kerry

Devon Dell, Galway

Hanora's Cottage, Nire Valley

• The Bridgestone 100 Best Places to Stay in Ireland is arranged **ALPHABETICALLY, BY COUNTY** so it begins with County Carlow, which is followed by County Cavan, and so on.

• Within the counties, the entries are once again listed alphabetically, so Aherne's, in Youghal, East Cork, is followed by Assolas House, in Kanturk, North Cork.

• Entries in Northern Ireland are itemised alphabetically, at the end of the book. All NI prices quoted in sterling.

• The contents of the Bridgestone 100 Best Guides are exclusively the result of the authors' deliberations. All meals and accommodation were paid for and any offers of discounts or gifts were refused.

• Many of the places featured in this book are only open during the summer season, which means that they can be closed for any given length of time between October and March. Many others change their opening times during the winter.

• **PRICES:** Average prices are calculated on the basis of one night's stay for bed and breakfast. Look out for special offers for weekends, several days' stay, or off season.

• **CREDIT CARDS:** Most houses take major credit cards, particularly the Visa, Access/Master group. Check if you intend to use American Express or Diners Card. If a house does not accept credit cards, this is indicated in the notes section of their entry.

• Finally, we greatly appreciate receiving reports, e-mails and criticisms from readers, and would like to thank those who have written in the past, whose opinions are of enormous assistance to us when considering which 100 places to stay finally make it into this book.

CONTENTS

CARLOW 20

CAVAN 23

CLARE 25

CORK 29

DONEGAL 49

DUBLIN 56

GALWAY 63

KERRY 76

KILKENNY 88

LAOIS 89

LEITRIM 91

LIMERICK 93

LOUTH 95

MAYO 96

MEATH 99

MONAGHAN 100

SLIGO 102

TIPPERARY 104

WATERFORD 106

WESTMEATH 115

WEXFORD 118

WICKLOW 121

NORTHERN IRELAND 123

INDEX 129

BARROWVILLE TOWNHOUSE

Randal & Marie Dempsey
Kilkenny Road
Carlow, County Carlow
Tel: (059) 914 3324
Fax: 914 1953
www.barrowvillehouse.com

Barrowville is peaceful, elegant and efficient, thanks entirely to the extra-hard work and careful consideration of Randal and Marie Dempsey.

It is the confident style of Barrowville Townhouse that we admire so much, the jazzy elegance that Randal and Marie bring to this fine old place, tucked in behind a perimeter wall as the road from Kilkenny to Carlow begins to head south.

And yet, unlike so many other addresses which force their style consciousness into self-consciousness, the Dempseys simply do things right. The house may be sleek, but above all it is comfortable, it is a place where you can relax from the second you walk in the door.

And Marie's breakfasts, served in the vine-clad conservatory which makes the most of the morning sunlight, again show not just style, but the careful consideration of a cook who knows that an Irish breakfast needs even more care in the choosing of ingredients than in the cooking of them. Attention to detail is the key to all the elements in Barrowville Townhouse, and explains how the house works so well, yet works so peaceably, so effectively.

- **OPEN:** All year
- **ROOMS:** Seven rooms, all en suite
- **PRICE:** B&B €75-€80 per double room, €50-€55 single room

- **NOTES:**
Visa, Master, Amex. No dinner. No wheelchair access. Private car parking. Children over 12 years welcome.

- **DIRECTIONS:**
On the right hand side after the traffic lights heading south out of Carlow. 50 miles from Dublin (Route N9); 50 miles from Rosslare (again N9).

KILGRANEY COUNTRY HOUSE

north

east

west

south

Bryan Leech & Martin Marley
Bagenalstown
County Carlow
Tel: (059) 977 5283 Fax: 977 5595
info@kilgraneyhouse.com
www.kilgraneyhouse.com

After a decade in business,
Bryan and Martin remain
at the cutting edge of
style, design and cooking.

Here's the problem. You want to stay in some of the newly converted courtyard suites at Kilgraney, because you want to see exactly what Bryan Leech and Martin Marley have achieved with their newest design challenge. And, these guys being two of the style icons of contemporary Ireland, you just must stay in these elegant covens of good taste: you have to be there!

But, then, you miss out on the chance to stay in this glamtastic house, one of the design glories of its age. And you miss out on Bryan's superb cooking, not to mention the embracing craic that develops around this dining room table as the evening moves on, the adrenaline of the guests powered by great flavours, and lovely wines.

Now, that is what we call a dilemma.

And we have no simple solution, save maybe taking the kids for a weekend of self-catering, which will introduce them to the lovely Barrow Valley, then maybe you can slip away together for a night or two on your own. Dilemmas!

- ● **OPEN:** Mar-Nov weekends, Jul-Aug weekly
- ● **ROOMS:** Six double, en suite rooms
- ● **PRICE:** B&B €45-€85 per person sharing. Weekend packages available. Self catering €350 per week.

● **NOTES:**
Visa, Master, Amex, Laser. Dinner 8pm €45, communal table, book by noon. Wheelchair access with assistance. Herbal treatments by appointment. Children over 12 only.

● **DIRECTIONS:**
Just off the R705, 3.5 miles from Bagenalstown (Muine Bheag) on the road heading towards Borris.

LORD BAGENAL INN

James & Mary Keogh
Leighlinbridge, County Carlow
Tel: (059) 972 1668
Fax: (059) 972 2629
info@lordbagenal.com
www.lordbagenal.com

James and Mary Keogh's pivotal Lord Bagenal Inn is becoming one of the vital escape haunts for weekending Dubliners, a place of calm respite.

Strolling around Leighlinbridge one fine summer day, admiring the flowers and the meticulous neatness of the streets and the public monuments, reminded us of being in a French village. The pride in their place which the good people of Leighlin take is inspiring.

Then we strolled in to have some lunch in the Lord Bagenal, and were inspired some more. Firstly by the extraordinary collection of modern Irish art which owner James Keogh has assembled over the years – you should go to Leighlin just to see these masterpieces – and then by the sane and civil service by the staff, the lovely food offered and served with charm, the relaxed and civilised ambience of these intimate rooms. This feeling of well-being explains why the Lord Bagenal is such a success, and such a fine place to stay: there is a calm civility about this address, about this village, that captures the nature of the Barrow Valley perfectly. It is distinctive, delightful, proud, a vital respite powered by local spirit.

- **OPEN:** All year, except Christmas Day
- **ROOMS:** 12 en suite bedrooms
- **PRICE:** B&B €55 midweek, €62.50 Fri/Sat per person sharing, single supplement €25 for bed and breakfast

- **NOTES:**
Carvery lunch. Afternoon bar menu. Evening bar menu from 6pm. Dinner from €35. Bar menu available. Limited wheelchair access. Private parking. Children welcome, playroom, babysitting.

- **DIRECTIONS:**
8 miles south of Carlow, signed off the main N9.

MacNEAN TOWNHOUSE

The Maguire family
Blacklion
County Cavan
Tel: (071) 985 3022
Fax: (071) 985 3404

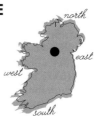

County Cavan is a borderland jewel which remains undiscovered. Make the MacNean your base, and get the best food as you find the best views.

One fine day in August 2003 we drove westwards through County Cavan, heading out of Sligo. At one point, we drove for almost 15 miles without seeing another moving vehicle: not even a tractor attending to silage or crops, far less a car driven by locals, far less a car with tourists. No one. Just sunshine billowing through tall hedgerows, just quiet lakes undisturbed by human endeavour, just narrow, lazy roads, and us.

This sort of escape from the madding crowds was possible in many places in Ireland 15 years ago. Today, it is hard to find, and it is this isolation that will be the future of Cavan: it is one of the last true escapes.

And, after your explorations, what is better than a simple room in The MacNean, and the promise of some of the finest contemporary cooking in Ireland from Neven Maguire and his team. This chef is a brilliant star, whose restaurant is packed at the weekends with city folk making a culinary pilgrimage. But don't rush back: slow down.

- **OPEN:** All year, except Christmas
- **ROOMS:** Five rooms
- **PRICE:** B&B €30-€35 per person sharing

- **NOTES:**
Visa, Mastercard. MacNean Bistro opens for Dinner, €55
Wheelchair access.
Children welcome.
Recommended for vegetarians.

- **DIRECTIONS:**
On the main street in Blacklion, which itself is just on the border with Northern Ireland.

THE OLDE POST INN

Tara McCann & Gearoid Lynch
Cloverhill, Butler's Bridge
County Cavan
Tel: (047) 55555 Fax: 55111
gearoidlynch@eircom.net
www.theoldepostinn.com

Tara and Gearoid are working extra-hard and cooking extra-hard, to make The Olde Post a success. They are getting there with gas in the tank.

A young couple running a restaurant with rooms, and putting body and soul into their work and their cooking, is one of those sights to melt a critic's heart. So it is with Tara and Gearoid in the sweet little Olde Post Inn in Cloverhill, a few miles out of Cavan town.

When they aren't packing them in at the weekends – book well in advance for Sunday lunch or you won't get a table – and running the place with great efficiency during the week, they are likely to have the paint brushes out doing up one of the rooms, or smartening up the dining rooms. This is a hands-on, do-everything operation, with two young people determined to make a success of their joint venture.

Mr Lynch's excellent, mature cookery is the secret ingredient of the OP: julienne of dover sole with asparagus is cheffy and clever, home-smoked guinea fowl with Puy lentils is splendid, whilst a warm mango tart is spot on. Book a room and make the most of this romantic spot.

- **OPEN:** all year, except Christmas
- **ROOMS:** seven rooms
- **PRICE:** B&B €38 per person
- **CREDIT CARDS:** All major cards accepted

- **NOTES:**
Wheelchair access. Children welcome.
Dinner 6.30pm-9.30pm Tue-Sat, 12.30pm-3pm, 6.30pm-9pm Sun, €40

- **DIRECTIONS:**
From Cavan follow N3. At Butlersbridge, take the N54 and the Olde Post is 3km further, on the right.

CLIFDEN HOUSE

Jim & Bernadette Robson
Corofin, County Clare
Tel: (065) 6837692
Fax: 6837692
www.clifdenhouse-countyclare.com
clifdenhousecountyclare@eircom.net

Some country houses are
theatrical, but Clifden is like a
great novel, a narrative of
human endeavour and history.

Clifden is one of our favourite country houses, and you will understand why we – and scores more like us – admire Jim and Bernadette Robson's place so much when you come and stay here, in this grand old pile hard by the lake on the edges of Corofin.

What everyone likes so much is the humour and sang-froid of the Robsons. They behave as if they are characters in a novel, which, in some ways, they are. Their story is bookended by their efforts with this house, by their struggle to maintain, improve and transform Clifden. The house itself provides the narrative – constantly demanding, constantly exasperating, constantly inspiring – and the Robson family play out their parts in the shadow of this louring, demanding, tempestuous monarch of mortar. Jim Robson provides the main storyline, and extemporises brilliantly; the man is a storyteller; Bernadette drops the asides. It is an altogether splendid entertainment: the great house, the great novel, the story of human hope.

- **OPEN:** Mar-end Oct
- **ROOMS:** Five rooms
- **PRICE:** B&B €65 per person sharing, €90 single

- **NOTES:**
Visa, Mastercard. Dinner, 8pm, €35, communal table. Private car parking. Two self-catering houses, sleep 6 or 8. Priced weekly. Children welcome. Two boats for guests.

- **DIRECTIONS:**
From the village of Corofin, turn left at the grotto, then take the second right. Their entranceway is the first right off this road.

FERGUS VIEW

Mary Kelleher
Kilnaboy, Corofin
County Clare
Tel: (065) 683 7606
Fax: 683 7192
deckell@indigo.ie

Comfort, comfort, comfort: that's the touchstone of Mary Kelleher's lovely B&B, just south of the beautiful Burren in beautiful County Clare.

The best places to stay in Ireland fit into our psyche as neatly as we fit into their comfy chairs and swaddlesome beds. So it is with Fergus View. Mary Kelleher's B&B is simple, straightforward, unpretentious, but the warmth of the welcome, the quality of the hospitality, the flavours of the cooking, and the comforting nature of the house, all combine to make it quite irresistible.

Mrs Kelleher does everything well, from tasty breakfasts that show real care in the cooking, to meticulous house-keeping that delights the eye, and she cooks lovely, domestic dinners that fizzle with the flavours of a good country cook. All in all, Fergus View makes complete sense as a place to base yourself if exploring the flora of the Burren: it's a house which you will leave with a contented tum in the morning, and to which you will be looking forward to returning to in the evening for a soulful, scrummy dinner and a sound night's sleep.

- **OPEN:** Easter-mid Oct
- **ROOMS:** Six rooms, five en suite
- **PRICE:** €34 per person sharing. Single room €46-€48

- **NOTES:**
No credit cards. Dinner for groups of six, Mon-Thur if pre-booked, 6.30pm (no dinner bank holidays). Dinner €24.50. No wheelchair access. Secure parking. Children welcome.

- **DIRECTIONS:**
From Ennis take the main road to Ennistymon but turn off to the right for Corofin after one mile. It is 2 miles north of Corofin on the road to Kilfenora.

MOY HOUSE

Antoin O'Looney
Lahinch
County Clare
Tel: (065) 708 2800 Fax: 708 2500
moyhouse@eircom.net
www.moyhouse.com

Moy House offers some of the most heart-stopping views of any Irish country house, whilst Bernie Merry makes sure everything else is 100%.

We tend to believe that it is counties Donegal and Kerry that offer the most spectacular displays of natural light and its endless permutations in Ireland.

Well, should you have the good fortune to spend an evening watching the light ebb and fade over Liscannor Bay, from the comfort of a lazy chair in the sitting room of Moy House – and preferably with a glass of hootch in hand – then you might reckon that the county Clare has something to say about that. For the dying of the light over Liscannor Bay is some sort of holy magic indeed.

Mind you, maybe it seems so impressive because you are so comfortable in the grand Moy House, which is so splendidly run by Bernie Merry. Great beds and sumptuous bathrooms, lovely cooking at breakfast, and the spirit of a country house meeting the spick and span of an hotel, all adds up to make Moy a great coastal destination. Make sure to book the rooms on the upper floor, and get ready for a light show of rare beauty.

- **OPEN:** Mid Jan-end Dec
- **ROOMS:** Nine rooms
- **PRICE:** €200-€229 double room, €127-€155 single.

- **NOTES:**
All major cards accepted.
Special offers Nov-May.
Group rates accepted. No dinner.

- **DIRECTIONS:**
Moy House is located about one mile south of Lahinch town, on the Miltown Malbay road. Shannon Airport is 1 hour's drive.

10 PLACES FOR
GREAT ROMANCE

1

THE BROOK LODGE
AUGHRIM, Co WICKLOW

2

CASTLE LESLIE
GLASLOUGH, Co MONAGHAN

3

THE CLARENCE
DUBLIN, Co DUBLIN

4

COAST
TRAMORE, Co WATERFORD

5

ISKEROON
CAHERDANIEL, Co KERRY

6

THE MOAT INN
TEMPLEPATRICK, NORTHERN IRELAND

7

THE MORRISON
DUBLIN, Co DUBLIN

8

SALVILLE HOUSE
ENNISCORTHY, Co WEXFORD

9

WINEPORT LODGE
GLASSAN, Co WESTMEATH

10

ZUNI
KILKENNY, Co KILKENNY

AHERNE'S

The Fitzgibbon family
163 North Main Street
Youghal, East Cork
Tel: (024) 92424 Fax: 93633
ahernes@eircom.net
www.ahernes.com

Superb good taste throughout the rooms, the restaurant and the bar is the Fitzgibbon family's signature in the ageless Aherne's of Youghal.

They have built the by-pass road around Youghal, a steep, up-hill-and-down job. It saves lots of time. Who cares? What sensible, food-loving traveller is going to detour around Youghal when Aherne's is there in the centre, beckoning you with its delicious food in both the bar and the restaurant, and with its comfortable, spacious rooms serving as a beacon of light for the tired traveller who wants to find some solace from the road. By-pass the town? Why would you do that.

Aherne's is tasteful in every way, from the super-efficient and personable service, led by the family members themselves, to the delicious cooking in the restaurant and bar, to the smart, stylish rooms. It is one of those addresses that works with ruthless efficiency and self-discipline to keep itself up to the mark, which means that Aherne's never dates, never goes out of fashion, remains always at the cutting edge. It is not just a staple of the Bridgestone Guides, but a staple of the best kind of Irish hospitality.

- **OPEN:** All year
- **ROOMS:** 12 rooms, all en suite
- **PRICE:** €70-€105 per person sharing, Single from €110

- **NOTES:**
Children welcome, 5-12yrs 50% reduction if sharing. Full wheelchair access. Secure parking. Dinner €42

- **DIRECTIONS:**
Youghal is on a one-way system, coming from Cork direction: when you get back onto the two-way system Aherne's Seafood Restaurant & Hotel is located 50 yards on the right-hand side – a yellow building.

ASSOLAS COUNTRY HOUSE

Joe & Hazel Bourke
Kanturk
North Cork
Tel: (029) 50015 Fax: 50795
assolas@eircom.net
www.assolas.com

From garden to kitchen is the Assolas House culinary mantra, and it is executed with winning sympathy.

Everything about the Bourke family's Assolas House has the measure of beauty. From the prim prettiness of the house itself, entwined in its beautiful grounds with a lazy stream lapping nearby, to the beautifully measured cooking that is the hallmark of Hazel Bourke's kitchen, everything in Assolas conspires to be enchanting.

The Bourkes talk of the 'symmetry' between kitchen and garden as being the pivot on which the cooking is founded, and Assolas enjoys the most direct relationship between what is produced in their fine walled garden, and what Hazel Bourke then creates in the kitchen. The simplicity of such a relationship, indeed, defines the simplicity of the cooking: St Tola goat's cheese custard with a roasted tomato sauce; duck with blackcurrant sauce; monkfish tail with a crust of garden herbs; duck confit with salad greens; chicken with a fresh tarragon sauce. But if the food reads modestly, its elegant profundity is stunning in its elaboration and display of flavour and texture.

- **OPEN:** Mid Mar-Nov
- **ROOMS:** Six rooms, all en suite
- **PRICE:** B&B €89-€130 per person sharing. Single supplement €16. 3rd person €45

- Dinner 7pm-8pm, €49. No wheelchair access. Private car park. Children welcome, under 5s sharing, free. Garden for children to play in.

- **DIRECTIONS:**
Take the N72 Mallow/Killarney road, and 10km west of Mallow you will see the first signpost. 33 miles from Cork airport (approx 1 hour).

BALLYMALOE HOUSE

The Allen family
Shanagarry
Midleton, East Cork
Tel: (021) 465 253, Fax: 465 2029
res@ballymaloe.ie
www.ballymaloe.com

Myrtle Allen is one of the truly significant, original and important figures of the 20th century.

In 2003, Myrtle Allen and her nephew, Cullen Allen, compiled a small handbook entitled 'Local producers of good food in Cork'. This was significant, because for the first time Mrs Allen was codifying the very thing that Ballymaloe House has been doing on a daily basis for more than 40 years, she was putting on paper the very philosophy that has made Ballymaloe one of the most celebrated food addresses in the world: local food produced by local people and eaten fresh in its locality. Here are the people who helped Mrs Allen create the unique Ballymaloe ethos, the Ballymaloe cuisine.

'Their produce is our treasure,' she writes, noting, 'They look for a living, not a fortune.' Of those who do look for a fortune, Mrs Allen's story about the smoked Denny hams tells all one needs to know about wealth, that is to say, true wealth versus transient wealth. Myrtle Allen understands true wealth, she makes art from the commonplace, she is one of the great figures of the century.

- ● **OPEN:** All year
- ● **ROOMS:** 34 rooms. No suites
- ● **PRICE:** B&B €96-€141 per person sharing. Single €110-€166. Spare bed €45

● **NOTES:**
All major credit cards accepted. Dinner 7pm-9.30pm, €55. Recommended for vegetarians. Children welcome, cot, high chair, early dinner. Private parking.

● **DIRECTIONS:**
From Cork take N25 to exit for Whitegate R630, follow signs for R629 Cloyne. House is 2 miles beyond Cloyne.

BALLYMAKEIGH HOUSE

**Margaret Browne
Killeagh, Co Cork
Tel: (024) 95184 Fax: 95370
ballymakeigh@eircom.net
www.ballymakeighhouse.com**

Excellent country cooking, good country comfort and a warm welcome make Ballymakeigh a very difficult place to bid farewell.

Margaret Browne is firmly back in the kitchen in Ballymakeigh, having leased her nearby restaurant, Browne's. She continues to enjoy her work, which explains why she is so good at it, and with the good cooking comes a chatty welcome which, with the laid-back style of the house, makes for a chill-out destination.

Good home baking – fine scones, lovely brown bread – introduces good country cooking: carrot and poppy seed soup, elderflower sorbet, salmon fillet on mashed potato, with generous helpings of vegetables; then nice sweet baking such as almond tartlets with cream and rhubarb. This is expert country cooking.

After such a feast you'll likely think you will never manage breakfast, but that is yet another extravaganza of baking and good savoury cooking: don't miss the fluffy omelettes with farmhouse cheese. And, somehow, you do manage to eat more than you would have believed. The comfort, welcome and cooking all make for an ace B&B.

● **OPEN:** Valentine weekend-1 Nov
● **ROOMS:** Six rooms, all en suite
● **PRICE:** B&B €50 per person, single supplement charged high season only, €10

● **NOTES:**
Amex, Visa, Mastercard accepted. Dinner 7.30pm-8.30pm, €37.50. No wheelchair access. Enclosed car park. Children welcome, high chair, cot, babysitting. 50% reduction for children when sharing a room.

● **DIRECTIONS:**
Signposted on the N25, 6 miles west of Youghal.

BALLYVOLANE

Merrie & Jeremy Green
Castlelyons
Fermoy, North Cork
Tel: (025) 36349 Fax: 36781
ballyvol@iol.ie
www.ballyvolanehouse.ie

One of the greatest of the
Irish country houses,
Ballyvolane is noble,
hospitable and loveable.

Ballyvolane is one of the great Irish country houses, and
it offers one of the great Irish country house experiences. Pitch up here – it's best to take the turning off the
N8 after you have passed through Rathcormac village,
going south – and you enter a little fairy tale of good living, a dream detour miles away from reality and the modern world as we know it.

The reason Ballyvolane works so well, and creates such
an enchantment, is precisely because Merrie and Jeremy
work so hard at their tasks. The attention to detail in
Ballyvolane – every single detail – is simply fantastic, in
particular the care taken with the cooking, which produces some of the best country house cooking in Ireland.
This excellent food, the great service, and the round-the-
table bonhommie it inspires amongst the contented
guests, is the centrepiece of the Ballyvolane escape, a delicious note to this step out of reality and into a delightful,
all-enveloping dreamscape.

- **OPEN:** 1 Jan-23 Dec
- **ROOMS:** Six rooms, all en suite
- **PRICE:** B&B €65-€85 per person. €20 single supple-
ment.

- **NOTES:**
Amex, Visa, Mastercard accepted. Dinner 8pm, €40, communal
table. Wheelchair access in one bedroom. Private car park.
Children welcome, high chair, cot. Self catering €400 per week.

- **DIRECTIONS:**
From the N8, south just after Rathcormac, take the turn
to Midleton and look for the sign for the house.

BARNABROW

Geraldine O'Brien
Cloyne, Midleton
East Cork
Tel: (021) 465 2534, Fax: 465 2534
barnabrow@eircom.net
www.barnabrowhouse.com

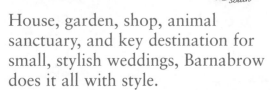

House, garden, shop, animal sanctuary, and key destination for small, stylish weddings, Barnabrow does it all with style.

Geraldine O'Brien's remarkable energy powers the sweet Barnabrow ever onwards. Style lovers crave this stylish, elegant house for its individuality and its beauty, for Mrs O'Brien has a meticulous eye for both colour and furnishings, keeping Barnabrow right up there with all the other immensely stylish houses which are such a feature of East Cork. This is the best sort of design, where fabrics and furnishings and colour schemes all conspire to create comfort, a comfort which envelopes you the minute you walk in the door.

But that is not all there is to this energised house, which also has a fine garden, an animal sanctuary, and a shop which sells African furniture that the O'Briens import. Barnabrow is also a key destination for local weddings, a dreamily romantic place in which to celebrate a betrothal in style. It's a little micro-universe, is Barnabrow, and more power to Mrs O'Brien's energy.

- **OPEN:** All year, except 24-28 Dec
- **ROOMS:** 19 en suite rooms
- **PRICE:** €55-€80 per person sharing. €20 single supplement.

- **NOTES:**
Restaurant serves lunch, €27, dinner, 7pm-9pm, €45. No wheelchair access. Secure parking. Children welcome - donkeys, goats, hens, ducks, geese.

- **DIRECTIONS:**
From N25 take Cloyne exit, turn left at Ballinacorra. Take Ballycotton road from Cloyne Cross, house is 2 miles out of village on left, before Ballymaloe House.

BLAIR'S COVE HOUSE

Philippe & Sabine de Mey
Durrus
Bantry
West Cork
Tel: (027) 61127, Fax: 61487
blairscove@eircom.net

The rooms and apartments in Blair's Cove are as stylish as it gets, so pamper yourself at the edge of lovely Dunmanus Bay in West Cork.

A friend described the dining room in Blair's Cove as being 'jaw dropping for those on a first visit'. That's absolutely true. This is one of the country's most beautiful, quietly spectacular, dining rooms, a gorgeous, high-ceilinged temple for eating. And on a first visit the romantic nature of the Blair's Cove location – the house sits on a promontory reaching out into lovely, unspoilt Dunmanus Bay, just south of Durrus village on the road heading south to Goleen – merely accentuates the stunning beauty of the whole experience.

Philippe and Sabine de Mey have had the good sense, then, to ensure that the rooms which adjoin the house are just as gorgeous as the location, and the restaurant. These are fantastically stylish places to stay, with a glamour and tactility that makes them hard to leave, and their design is hugely effective and comforting. Do note that the apartments can be rented for self catering, should you be seeking a West Cork base for touring the peninsulas.

● **OPEN:** Mar-Nov
● **ROOMS:** Three courtyard suites, one cottage in grounds
● **PRICE:** B&B €85-€100 per person sharing. Single supplement €30

● **NOTES:**
All major cards accepted. Restaurant serves dinner, Tue-Sat, €50. Children welcome. Self-catering cottage.

● **DIRECTIONS:**
1.5km outside the village of Durrus on the Barleycove/Mizen Head road. Look for the blue gates.

HOUSE

...ve Coakley
Blindgate, Kinsale
West Cork
Tel: (021) 477 7858, Fax: 477 7868
info@blindgatehouse.com
www.blindgatehouse.com

One of the most sensual
and inspiring houses,
Blindgate has perfect feng
shui: just feel it!

Maeve Coakley's Blindgate House is one of those places that makes you feel fantastic. The design of this dream destination is so acutely achieved – Ms Coakley worked with the interior designer Beatrice Blake to great effect – that it lifts your spirits just to walk in the door.

The feng shui of the public rooms and the bedrooms is so pitch perfect that it achieves a positively sensual effect. This is a most tactile house, an address where fabrics, furnishings, art works and hospitality all commingle to give the customer what feels like nothing less than an arresting big hug of comfort.

You can only achieve this sort of effect by being fiercely motivated, and the determination to achieve ever-better standards is just as evident in Ms Coakley's cooking at breakfast as it is in the design of the house. Once again, this cooking has a luxurious sensuality to it, thanks to freshness, judgement, dammit, thanks to simple good taste. Blindgate House makes you feel like a million dollars.

● **OPEN:** Mar-Dec
● **ROOMS:** 11 rooms (seven twin rooms, three standard double rooms & one superior double)
● **PRICE:** B&B €115-€170 per room

● **NOTES:**
Visa, Mastercard, Amex. No dinner. Wheelchair access with assistance, but no walk-in showers. Ample enclosed parking. No children under 8 years.

● **DIRECTIONS:**
200m past St Multose Church – just up the hill from the Fishy Fishy café.

BOW HALL

Dick & Barbara Vickery
Castletownshend
West Cork
Tel: (028) 36114
dvicbowhall@eircom.net

How does the amazing
Barbara Vickery manage to
do all she does? Don't know,
but we're sure grateful.

We don't want anyone to accuse us of ageism over what
follows, but we have to be honest, and explain our quizzi-
cality: Barbara Vickery, major-D of the very lovely Bow
Hall, has seen four score years come and go, and we just
don't know how she does what she does. We don't know.
What we do know is: we are sure grateful.

What Mrs Vickery does is to marshal this house with the
command of a lieutenant, and the zip of a teenager, cooking smashing breakfasts for guests, keeping her trio of
Shaker-style rooms in tip-top shape, and all the time creating a vibe about this dreamy house that is simply irresistible. It's an idyllic place, and exactly the sort of house
you want to find in a charming village like
Castletownshend: relaxed, relaxing, stylish in an ageless
way. Ageless is just the right word, come to think of it. Mrs
Vickery and her house have an ageless energy and brio
that is the very soul of hospitality itself, and age or ageism
simply doesn't come into it: Bow Hall has the life force.

- **OPEN:** All year, except Christmas
- **ROOMS:** Three rooms, all with private baths
- **PRICE:** €45 per person sharing, Single supplement €5

- **NOTES:**
No smoking house. No credit cards accepted. Dinner
8pm, €30, communal table, by reservation only.
No wheelchair access. Enclosed car park.
Children welcome, high chair, cot.

- **DIRECTIONS:**
On the right hand side of the village, heading down the
steep hill.

FORTVIEW HOUSE

Violet Connell
Gurtyowen
Toormore, Goleen
West Cork
Tel & Fax: (028) 35324
fortviewhousegoleen@eircom.net

Everyone's favourite West
Cork B&B, Fortview is a
truly fantastic farmhouse
getaway.

If you need to understand why Fortview is so special, perhaps a clue to the vision that drives Violet and Richard
Connell's farm and bed and breakfast lies here.

During the 2003 season of farm walks in West Cork,
organised by the Growing Awareness group, the Connell's
farm was included amongst the other roster of farms that
are run organically. 'Beef dairy farm in a scenic location
with some interesting planting of hedgerows and trees
and a reed bed system', the blurb says laconically. The significant thing is that Fortview is not an organic farm, such
farms being the traditional focus of farm walks. But what
Fortview is is a meticulously managed farm, an example of
the skills and crafts of farm practice at their best. And
what Richard does on the farm, Violet does with the B&B:
meticulous management, quiet application, studied
resolve, a pleasure in the work at hand. All of this has
made Fortview one of the best-loved B&B's in Ireland, a
beacon of best practice, and the most delicious cooking.

- ● **OPEN:** 1 March-1 Nov
- ● **ROOMS:** Five rooms, all en suite
- ● **PRICE:** B&B €40 per person sharing

● **NOTES:**
Dinner by arrangement only. Self-catering house
available, sleeps six. No wheelchair access.
Enclosed car park.
Children over 6 years welcome.

● **DIRECTIONS:**
Signposted 2km from Toormore on the main Durrus
road (R591). 12km from Durrus, 9km from Goleen.

GARNISH HOUSE

Con & Hansi Lucey
Western Road
Cork City, County Cork
Tel: (021) 427 5111 Fax: 427 3872
garnish@iol.ie
www.garnish.ie

Garnish House is garnished with the endless solicitude of Hansi Lucey, a solicitude that no one who stays here can fail to be completely charmed by.

There is a gentleness, a solicitousness, a sweetness about the Cork character that is unique in Ireland, and, for us, Mrs Hansi Lucey of Garnish House, Western House, Cork city, embodies that very spirit: you just can't imagine her working anywhere other than Cork city.

Her kindness, then, is the very animus of this house, and it is, after you have been here about two minutes, the only thing that you will notice. The endless solicitude at breakfast time, as Hansi fusses over you to make sure you have absolutely everything you could need or want, is awesome, and you set out with a spring in your step, inspired by such abundant generosity.

In all the years we have been staying at Garnish, we have never known anyone to be other than completely charmed by this lady. And, every single year, the letters of praise pour in from delighted folk who have finally found this 'gem' (for some reason, they always call it a gem). Actually, the reason they call it a gem is because it's a gem.

- **OPEN:** All year
- **ROOMS:** 14 rooms, all en suite
- **PRICE:** B&B €40-€75 per person, €55-75 single

- **NOTES:**
No dinner. Limited wheelchair access.
Enclosed car parking. Children welcome, high chair, cot, babysitting, reduction if sharing. Self-catering suites available.

- **DIRECTIONS:**
Five minutes' walk from the city centre, just opposite UCC.

GLENALLY HOUSE

Fred & Herta Rigney
Copperalley, Youghal
East Cork
Tel: (024) 91623
enquiries@glenally.com
www.glenally.com

One of the key addresses
for style lovers, Glenally
fuses old style and new
style quite brilliantly.

A pair of striking people, who have together created one
of the most strikingly beautiful houses in Ireland. That is
Fred and Herta Rigney and their gorgeous Glenally
House, one of the interior design jewels of our day.
Right from the outset, when they toured Ireland looking
for the right place, the Rigneys always wanted 'a place to
play around with, something to work on'. Glenally has had
their meticulous eyes trained on it with fabulous success,
creating a remarkable synthesis that fuses their love of
modern style with their love of old houses. Making those
elements work together is the brilliance of Glenally: lean
Italian furniture with Georgian colours, old light cornices
with modern lights – they have a thing about lights – the
amalgamation of modern bathrooms into old bedrooms.
It's a peach of a place, a comfort zone further underlined
by their welcome and their serious interest in cooking.
The Rigneys are autodidactic: give them a challenge, and
they rise to it and they master it. See that mastery here.

- **OPEN:** 1 Mar-mid Dec. Reservations only Dec-Feb
- **ROOMS:** Four rooms, 3 all en suite, 1 private bath
- **PRICE:** B&B €45-€60 per person sharing, €15 single
supplement.

- **NOTES:**
Visa, Mastercard. Dinner, 8pm, €40. No wheelchair
access. Secure car parking. No facilities for under 12s.

- **DIRECTIONS:**
From roundabout east of Clockgate, continue straight
on N25 past Esso, 250m, take first left. After 75m turn
right and go to end of lane (200m) and through gates.

10 WEEKENDING PLACES
FOR DUBLINERS

1

BALLYKNOCKEN HOUSE
ASHFORD, Co WICKLOW

2

BALLYVOLANE HOUSE
FERMOY, Co CORK

3

BROOK LODGE INN
AUGHRIM, Co WICKLOW

4

GHAN HOUSE
CARLINGFORD, Co LOUTH

5

HANORA'S COTTAGE
NIRE VALLEY, Co WATERFORD

6

KILGRANEY HOUSE
BAGENALSTOWN, Co CARLOW

7

LORD BAGENAL
LEIGHLINBRIDGE, Co CARLOW

8

OLDE POSTE INN
BUTLER'S BRIDGE, Co CAVAN

9

ROUNDWOOD HOUSE
MOUNTRATH, Co LAOIS

10

WINEPORT LODGE
GLASSAN, Co WESTMEATH

GROVE HOUSE

Billy & Mary O'Shea
Colla Road, Schull
West Cork
Tel: (028) 28067, Fax: 28069
billyoshea@yahoo.com
www.grovehouseschull.com

Grove is a model B&B in every way: great style, great comfort, great cooking and superb hospitality bundle the visitor up in sheer, simple pleasure.

Billy and Mary O'Shea have that elusive decorator's eye, that innate skill that allows someone to use a bricolage of effects in a house, and to somehow bring all these effects together to create an interior that has real panache. Strong deep colours, abstract canvases, pitch pine floors and lots of period effects all work their magic in Grove House, an address fast acquiring a reputation not merely as the place to stay in lovely Schull, but also as a real style lover's retreat, an address to place alongside the other design jewels in this book.

But the O'Shea's painstaking application means that the interior is simply one part of this operation to have been deeply considered. The cooking is wisely based around West Cork artisan products, featuring brilliant foods from bacon to smoked salmon to still-warm hen's eggs, which makes for a breakfast that is a rare treat; don't miss those specially-made sausages. And great hospitality brings the whole happy shebang of Grove House seamlessly in tune.

- **OPEN:** Mar-Oct
- **ROOMS:** Five double rooms
- **PRICE:** B&B €50-€65 per person sharing. Single supplement €25

- **NOTES:**
No restaurant (plenty locally). No wheelchair access. Private parking. Not suitable for children under 12.

- **DIRECTIONS:**
Drive through village of Schull to the library. Take left turn onto Colla Road, Grove House is about 500 metres on the right-hand side.

LONGUEVILLE HOUSE

**The O'Callaghan family
Mallow
North Cork
Tel: (022) 47156, Fax: 47459
info@longuevillehouse.ie
www.longuevillehouse.ie**

To stay and eat at Longueville gives some idea of the holistic magnificence and abundance of rural Ireland.

Longueville House is the only Double Icon destination in the Bridgestone Guides, an address which is peerless for cooking and hospitality. Remarkably, it has won little attention beyond those in Ireland who love the outrageously creative cooking of William O'Callaghan, a curious fact given the astronomic standards achieved in this pink, pretty, storybook house.

But, then, the O'Callaghans are quiet country folk, unconcerned with the media, and they do things in their subtle, understated way, satisfying their own demand for constant improvements. The house, with its superb walled garden, its apple trees, its vineyard, its farm and outhouses, is an empire unto itself, and like true country folk, the O'Callaghans respect their land and what it produces, and they know how to get the very best out of it. To stay and eat here is to get a concept of the holistic magnificence and the abundant generosity of which rural Ireland is capable. Longueville is not just a Double Icon: it's a dream.

- **OPEN:** Mar-Nov
- **ROOMS:** 20 rooms, all en suite
- **PRICE:** B&B €180-€260 per room. Supplements apply for superior rooms and suites.

- **NOTES:**
Dinner served from 6.30pm, €50. Recommended for special diets. No wheelchair access. Children welcome, babysitting on request, toy chest, working farm.

- **DIRECTIONS:**
3 miles west of Mallow on the N72 to Killarney. Look for the large sign.

OTTO'S CREATIVE CATERING

Otto & Hilda Kunze
Dunworley, Butlerstown
Bandon, West Cork
Tel: (023) 40461
ottokunze@eircom.net
www.ottoscreativecatering.com

The holistic vision of hospitality embraced by Otto and Hilda at the remote, sea-swept OCC is powerful and profound, and unforgettable.

Certain people have thought so deeply about the concept of hospitality, cooking and entertainment, that the way in which they offer these services becomes completely radical, utterly individual. Myrtle Allen of Ballymaloe House is one of those people. Ken Buggy, Paddy Foyle and Bill Kelly are some other Irish mavericks. And Otto and Hilda Kunze are another pair of radical revolutionaries, people whose entire vision of hospitality and cooking is completely distinctive, completely their own.

OCC is not like any other place to stay and eat. The vision Otto and Hilda have is completely holistic: you don't go to OCC, you escape to it, you liberate yourself from the normal world to be at this simple but vital spa for the soul in wild, wonderful, sea-swept Dunworley, where the power of the sea seems more elemental than anywhere else on the south coast. Combined with the astonishing cooking, this retreat for the senses will leave you feeling not just rejuvenated, but feeling re-born.

● **OPEN:** All year
● **ROOMS:** Two double rooms and self-catering cottage
● **PRICE:** B&B €50 per person sharing, €20 single supplement.
● **CREDIT CARDS:** Visa, Mastercard.

● **NOTES:**
Dinner served Wed-Sat, €45, Sun lunch €30. No wheelchair access. Secure parking. Children welcome.

● **DIRECTIONS:**
From Bandon go to Timoleague, follow signs to Barryroe until you come across signs to Dunworley.

ROCK COTTAGE

Barbara Klotzer
Barnatonicane, Schull
West Cork
Tel & Fax: (028) 35538
rockcottage@eircom.net
www.mizen.net/rockcottage

One of the great West Cork escapes, Barbara Klotzer's elegant house isn't actually a cottage, but a stylish, pristine Georgian farmhouse hideaway.

Rock Cottage is a serious misnomer, for Barbara Klotzer's fine address is, in fact, an elegant Georgian, two-storey, slate-fronted house, dating from 1826, and its swish interior style is modern and European, rather than country-cottagey traditional.

But Rock Cottage does ring true, it does sound right, for this is a great place to escape to, far down the Mizen peninsula – it's almost in Goleen – and the get-away-from-it-all feel of the house is best shown by the fact that Ms Klotzer has guests staying all year, and that her splendid self-catering cottage is booked up all year long.

The detail shown in the house is even more evident in the cooking at breakfast and at dinner, which uses McCarthy's beef from Bantry, Barbara's own lamb from the farm, Roscarbery pork, Sally Barnes' fantastic smoked fish from Castletownshend, all the great, true tastes of West Cork. If you need to escape the madding crowd, then there is really nowhere better than Rock Cottage.

- **OPEN:** All year
- **ROOMS:** Three rooms and self-catering cottage
- **PRICE:** B&B €90-€110 per person sharing, €69-€75 single.

- **NOTES:**
Visa, Mastercard. Dinner, 7.30pm, book 24hrs ahead, €35, Children welcome, cot, working farm.

- **DIRECTIONS:**
From Schull, go west towards Goleen. At Toormore turn right onto the R591 towards Durrus. After 1.5 miles you will see their sign on the left.

SEA VIEW HOUSE HOTEL

Kathleen O'Sullivan
Ballylickey, Bantry
West Cork
Tel: (027) 50462 Fax: 51555
info@seaviewhousehotel.com
www.seaviewhousehotel.com

One of the best-loved small hotels you can find in Ireland, Sea View is driven by the hard work of Kathleen O'Sullivan and her devoted team.

Kathleen O'Sullivan knows that God is in the detail, and that scriptural urgency is the animus behind the lovely Sea View House Hotel. Everything that one might expect of a small, intimate, country hotel is raised – and maintained – at a sparkling standard, thanks to the driven work of Ms O'Sullivan and her team. They work hard, harder than anyone else, we reckon.

Sea View is one of those rare addresses which taps into our subconscious, because we all have a romantic, nostalgic concept of just what a small, owner-run West Cork country hotel should be like. We want it warm and welcoming, decorated in the classic style, comfortable in a quiet way, with generous country cooking. But Ms O'Sullivan goes one step further, she trumps our subconscious, for Sea View is warmer, more welcoming, more intimate, more expected, than we dared to expect. The attention to every detail in every aspect gladdens the heart, and creates the little country hotel of our dreams.

- **OPEN:** mid Mar-mid Nov
- **ROOMS:** 25 rooms
- **PRICE:** B&B €120-€175 per room

- **NOTES:**
All major cards accepted. Dinner in restaurant 7pm-9pm, Sun lunch (from Easter Sun) and lounge food daily. Dinner €40.
Full wheelchair access. Secure parking.

- **DIRECTIONS:**
On the N71 from Cork, 3 miles from Bantry and 8 miles from Glengarriff.

THE SLIP WAY

Wilmie Owen
The Cove, Baltimore
Co Cork
Tel: (028) 20134 Fax: 20134
theslipway@hotmail.com
www.theslipway.com

Just across from the water's edge in
sweet little Baltimore, Wilmie Owen's
little B&B is cute, but make sure to
book the rooms with the sea views.

A fine summer's morning and, after a stroll up the hill to
view the Beacon and to take a look out across to Sherkin
Island, you are sitting on the garden seat in The Slipway,
looking out across pretty little Baltimore harbour, with its
boats lined up neatly in the water.

A peaceful, slow morning, as you recall a stupendous dinner the previous evening in The Customs House in the
village. A bright, sea-breezy, sun-shiny day beckons, and
your appetite has been primed by the walk for one of the
excellent breakfasts prepared by Wilmie in the upstairs
room. Well, this is just as good as it gets, in the West Cork
way. Bring me back to Baltimore.

The harbour-facing rooms in The Slipway are simple,
spare and uncluttered, with small shower rooms, but this
simplicity feels right. Breakfasts are a delight: fine scrambled eggs with smoked salmon, lovely breads and crois-
sants; fine kippers, good coffee and tea, and more amazing views. Simple and sweet, and great value for money.

- **OPEN:** Mar-Nov
- **ROOMS:** Four rooms, all shower only
- **PRICE:** B&B from €31-€34 per person sharing, sin-
gle supplement €50-60

- **NOTES:**
No credit cards. No dinner.
No wheelchair access.
Not suitable for children under 12yrs

- **DIRECTIONS:**
Travel through Baltimore, to the Cove, and you will see
the sign, overlooking the Cove.

TRAVARA LODGE

Brendan Murphy & Richard May
Courtmacsherry
West Cork
Tel: (023) 46493
travaralodge@eircom.net

'We're not here for a long time: we're
here for a good time' is Richard May's
cheery motto. That good time is guar-
anteed at the vivacious Travara.

Overlooking the cove at Courtmacsherry ('Courtmac' if
you want to sound like a local), Travara Lodge is pretty,
unpretentious, and its promise of a quintessential West
Cork experience is more than delivered by owners
Brendan Murphy and Richard May.

The fact that it takes a couple of Dublin guys to know
how to deliver a real West Cork experience is something
you will have to figure out for yourselves. But, we sin-
cerely recommend that you do, indeed. Go Figure!

The rooms are simple, but details such as fresh wild flowers, good water glasses and pristine housekeeping are
what counts. Downstairs, the tiny dining room is the epi-
centre of West Cork craic, with Mr May directing the
room like a circus master. Brendan Murphy's cooking is
very fine – don't miss the crab cakes, and the wild salmon
with spinach is superlative, as are desserts – whilst service has a sassy charm that is irresistible. Wine buffs can't
miss the bottles imported by local man Tony Staunton.

- **OPEN:** All year, except the month of Oct
- **ROOMS:** Six rooms
- **PRICE:** B&B €40 per person sharing

- **NOTES:**
All major cards accepted
Wheelchair access.
Children welcome.
Dinner, 6.30pm-9.30pm, €40 per person

- **DIRECTIONS:**
The house is overlooking the bay in the centre of the
village.

CASTLE MURRAY HOUSE HOTEL

Marguerite Howley
Dunkineely, County Donegal
Tel: (074) 973 7022
castlemurray@eircom.net
www.castlemurray.com

The archetypal Irish restaurant with rooms powers ahead under Marguerite Howley and her young, friendly and hard-working team.

Castle Murray calls itself an hotel, but the fact of the matter is that it's truthfully a restaurant with rooms, in which guise it is the archetype of such places in Ireland. The rooms are simple, and inexpensive, and their prime function is to allow you to make the most of the restaurant, where you will enjoy spirited seafood cookery, whilst at the same time swooning over some of the most heavenly scenery you can enjoy.

But Castle Murray offers more than that simple recipe of rooms and restaurant. For this is a supremely relaxing place, one of the best chill-out zones you can find. The fact of its magical location is just one element that makes Castle Murray so fine, and the staff are another, and the excellent cookery brings all of these things back home. So, order up that g'n't, decide to have the steamed McSwayne's bay lobster, with maybe the ever-popular prawns and monkfish in garlic butter to start, and let the elemental; beauty of Castle Murray steep into your soul.

- ● **OPEN:** All year
- ● **ROOMS:** Ten rooms
- ● **PRICE:** B&B €58-€70 per person sharing. Single €80

- ● **NOTES:**
Visa, Mastercard. Restaurant open 7pm-9.30pm Mon-Sat, 1.30pm-3.30pm, 6.30pm-8.30pm Sun, Dinner €35-€46, Sun Lunch €22.50 No wheelchair access. Children welcome.

- ● **DIRECTIONS:**
Dunkineely is west of Donegal town, and Castle Murray is signposted just west of the village, on the N56 road from Donegal to Killybegs.

COXTOWN MANOR

Edward Dewael
Laghey
County Donegal
Tel: (074) 973 4574, Fax: 973 4576
coxtownmanor@oceanfree.net
www.coxtownmanor.com

With new rooms being added, Ed Dewael's Coxtown is powering into the new century on the crest of great hospitality and great service.

We have a fine old book written by Ruth van Waerebeek, entitled 'Everyone Eats Well In Belgium Cookbook' Sounds unlikely? Not a bit. 'Belgian food is cause for celebration', wrote the late, great Richard Olney in the rear of the book, and Ed Dewael's cooking in Coxtown drives the point home with delicious certainty. Belgian cooks understand how to get the best out of their ingredients, and so the folk of Donegal are lucky to have this fine chef transforming pristine local fish and shellfish, beef and lamb and game into serene, accomplished cooking.

In fact, what Mr Dewael has done so well is to unify a precise European culinary heritage with a laid-back Donegal ambience, and together the two make Coxtown some sort of peach. Don't miss the fish cookery, particularly the john dory cooked Belgian style, don't miss the chocolate desserts or the Belgian beers, and do stay a night in the cosy rooms and enjoy a smart, well-considered breakfast that brings staying in Coxtown to a fine conclusion.

● **OPEN:** All year, except early spring
● **ROOMS:** Ten rooms
● **PRICE:** B&B €55-€80 per person sharing. Single supplement €19. Gourmet breaks available, dinner plus B&B rates quoted.

● **NOTES:**
Visa, Mastercard, Laser. Dinner, 7pm-9pm, à la carte menu. Children welcome - family rooms.

● **DIRECTIONS:**
Look for their sign on the N15 between Ballyshannon and Donegal, turning just before the Esso station.

CROAGHROSS

John & Kay Deane
Portsalon, Letterkenny
County Donegal
Tel: (074) 915 9548 Fax: 915 9546
jkdeane@croaghross.com
www.croaghross.com

John and Kay are one of the great double acts in Irish hospitality, swopping tasks as to the manner born, and making Croaghross a great escape.

Maybe it's because John and Kay Deane are such a fantastic hospitality double-act, effortlessly alternating the multiple tasks of meeting and greeting, cooking and serving, that explains why the delightful Croaghross has such a vivid sense of energy, such an animated spirit. This pair make a fine team, and make a fine destination.

Then again, with the wild Donegal winds whipping up the hill to Croaghross from the awesome – and we mean awesome – Portsalon strand, who wouldn't be fired-up with energy? That fresh air, that extraordinary view down to the strand, is inspiring, intoxicating, a blast of pure elemental naturalism that roars elementally into your soul. Best of all, after you have allowed the winds and the waves to rip into your soul, there is some seriously good cooking for dinner: marinated lamb baked in puff pastry; the Sophie Grigson-inspired cod with crème fraîche and tomatoes; plaice with coriander and ginger; roasted vegetables; avocado cheesecake, and some lovely wines. Ace.

- **OPEN:** Mar-Oct (off season by arrangement)
- **ROOMS:** 5 double rooms, 3 en suite, 2 with showers.
- **PRICE:** €35-50 per person sharing, Single suppl. €6.50

- **NOTES:**
All major cards. Dinner Fri & Sat, €27.50. Light meals available Sun-Thur. Children welcome, high tea by arrangement. Self-catering cottage. Full wheelchair access.

- **DIRECTIONS:**
In Portsalon, turn right at crossroads, continue past church and golf course, take small road on left, house half mile on left.

THE GREEN GATE

Paul Chatenoud
Ardvally
Ardara
County Donegal
Tel: (074) 954 1546

The bewitching Green Gate is a taste of the Ireland of old in its almost-Spartan simplicity. It's a place where you can let your soul breathe.

This isn't a statistically based assertion, but we would reckon that for every dozen visitors to Paul Chatenoud's Green Gate, there are a couple who not only don't get what it is that makes the GG special, but who are positively affronted by the spartan simplicity of M. Chatenoud's little collection of cottages.

But, they would say, this is what we have left behind, this is the Ireland of old that we have struggled to separate ourselves from, this is the Ireland of peace dropping slowly, of contemplation, of time moving at time's pace, the Ireland of a material simplicity that we don't want anymore. And they probably turn their car (doubtless a well-polished 4x4) around and head back down the hill.

But, for those who do get what it is that this simple, elegant, ageless little collection of cottages offers, you simply can't get enough of its monastic calm, its space in time, its understanding of what it is in life, and indeed in hospitality, that is important. The Green Gate is Ireland of old.

● **OPEN:** All year
● **ROOMS:** Four rooms, all en suite
● **PRICE:** B&B €30-€40 per person

● **NOTES:**
No dinner. No credit cards.
Wheelchair access.
Private parking.
Children welcome.

● **DIRECTIONS:**
A mile east of Ardara, way, way up the hill, and signposted from the road.

10 NEW
DISCOVERIES

1

BALLYMAKEIGH HOUSE
KILLEAGH, Co CORK

2

CARRIG HOUSE
RING OF KERRY, Co KERRY

3

COAST TOWNHOUSE
TRAMORE, Co WATERFORD

4

THE COURTHOUSE
KINLOUGH, Co LEITRIM

5

IVERNA COTTAGE
SPIDDAL, Co GALWAY

6

MERRION HALL
DUBLIN, Co DUBLIN

7

THE OLDE POSTE INN
BUTLER'S BRIDGE, Co CAVAN

8

THE SLIPWAY
BALTIMORE, Co CORK

9

STELLA MARIS
BALLYCASTLE, Co MAYO

10

TRAVARA LODGE
COURTMACSHERRY, Co CORK

THE MILL

Derek and Susan Alcorn
Figart, Dunfanaghy
County Donegal
Tel & Fax: (074) 913 6985
info@themillrestaurant.com
www.themillrestaurant.com

Great value, great cooking, and a drop-dead location means The Mill has been a big hit from the day Derek and Susan first opened their doors.

Splendid cooking, superb value for money, and a profound professionalism have ensured the success of The Mill, right from the first day Susan and Derek Alcorn opened their doors. The mix of attractions is congratulated by the splendidly designed rooms – the artist Frank Eggington, whose house and studio this was, would have been delighted with such restraint and such a sure eye for colour and detail – and by the fabulous natural beauty of the area: book early and make sure you secure a room with views out across New Lake, for the sunsets are superlatively beautiful.

And a pivotal key to their success has been the excellent value for money of both dinner and accommodation, a fact that has been bringing the punters back from day one. This ability to balance everything, and to make it all work with such seeming ease, explains the sure-footed style of The Mill. Go once, and you will back again quickly to let a little more of that Donegal magic into your life.

- **OPEN:** Easter-Hallowe'en, open every night
- **ROOMS:** Six rooms
- **PRICE:** B&B €40 per person sharing. Single €50

- **NOTES:**
Visa, Mastercard, Amex. Restaurant open Tue-Sun, dinner, €34. No wheelchair access.
Children welcome - children's menu, travel cot, babysitting if needed.

- **DIRECTIONS:**
From L'kenny, take N56 through Dunfanaghy. The Mill is a half mile past the village, on the right, beside the lake.

ROSSAOR HOUSE

Brian & Anne Harkin
Ballyliffin, Inishowen
County Donegal
Tel & Fax: (074) 937 6498
rossaor@gofree.indigo.ie
www.ballyliffin.com/rossaor.htm

Brian and Anne's super-comfy B&B is just where you want to be in Inishowen, whether golfing or painting, or just chilling out is your ambition.

Rossaor is an Irish B&B as Irish B&B's should be: welcoming hosts, fine comfortable bedrooms and public rooms, and grand, delicious, glorious breakfasts. To be perfectly honest, Rossaor is so comfortable, so swaddling, that it takes a fair act of will, after a lazy, lingering breakfast, to actually get yourself up and running and out of the doors into that magical, surrounding landscape. Brian and Anne look after everyone so well that virtually everyone who stays at Rossaor is a regular visitor, a convert to their way of doing things.

Inishowen is a magnet for landscape painters, artistic souls with easels and palettes and a determination to capture the wildly elusive patterns of light that bless this beautiful part of the country. But, even if you lack the easel and the palette, you owe it to yourself to have a few days in the company of this mesmerising – and we don't use that word lightly – landscape, and your destination, then, should be Rossaor. Spoil yourself. You're worth it.

- **OPEN:** All year, except Christmas and New Year
- **ROOMS:** 4 rooms, all en suite, (incl 3 family rooms)
- **PRICE:** €40 per person sharing. Single supplement €10

- **NOTES:**
Mastercard, Visa. No dinner. Partial wheelchair access (a couple of steps at main entrance). Private car parking. Children accepted, but no facilities.

- **DIRECTIONS:**
From Buncrana follow R238 to Clonmany, Ballyliffin is 1.5 miles further on, still on the R238. House is about 100 yards past the Strand Hotel, on the left.

ABERDEEN LODGE

Pat Halpin
53-55 Park Avenue
Ballsbridge, Dublin 4
Tel: (01) 283 8155 Fax: 283 7877
aberdeen@iol.ie
www.halpinsprivatehotels.com

Excellent staff who genuinely care about the comfort and welfare of their guests means that Aberdeen Lodge is always packed with regular customers.

Sharply focused service from smiling staff, and a true feeling of a relaxing-away-from-it-all destination, are the keynotes of the success of Pat Halpin's Aberdeen Lodge, a well-renovated and well-maintained Edwardian house in sedate Ballsbridge.

The biscuits are home-made and the plunger coffee is freshly brewed for you on arrival, the breakfasts show real care in the cooking, especially the buffet of fruit salads and breads, mueslis and juices. If the rooms are slightly conventional, with their pale palette of colours, they are never less than comfortable, especially the standard rooms which win out in style over the period furniture and four-posters that are used in the larger suites.

Aberdeen is frequently filled with regular customers, which is probably the best recommendation you can make for the house: people come here once, and they come back again, and again, because you are so well looked after in this calm, sophisticated and elegant house.

- ● **OPEN:** All year
- ● **ROOMS:** 17 rooms, including two suites
- ● **PRICE:** €65-€90 per person sharing, €99-€120 single

● **NOTES:**
Light 'drawing room' menu, €8-€15 per course, extensive wine list. Secure parking.
Wheelchair access.
Children - not suitable for children under 7yrs.

● **DIRECTIONS:**
Just down from the Sydney Parade DART station. Park Avenue runs parallel with Merrion Road & Strand Road.

BROWNE'S

Barry J Canny
22 St Stephen's Green, Dublin 2
Tel: **(01) 638 3939**
Fax: **(01) 638 3900**
brownesdublin@eircom.net
www.brownesdublin.com

The new alliance between Barry
Canny's townhouse hotel and the Stein
Group, which specialises in boutique
hotels, augurs well for Browne's.

Barry Canny has merged his successful city centre hotel
with Spain's Stein Group, which enfolds Browne's into its
current portfolio of eight hotels, scattered throughout
Europe. But Stein has plans to open a further 15 boutique
hotels in the short period, so one can expect some
dynamism from this alliance: certainly the standards
achieved by Browne's could be replicated successfully in
many other cities in Ireland, for this has been a singularly
well maintained and creative little hotel and restaurant.

Mr Canny remains a director of Browne's, but has already
turned his attention to a new St Stephen's Green project,
Peploe's, six doors down from Browne's.

Peploe's has been two years in the planning – Mr Canny
is nothing if not thorough – and will be a swish wine bar
serving beagies and also an à la carte menu, and will feature a viniculture library.

But Browne's remains one of the best Dublin addresses,
thanks to a great location and attentive, responsive staff.

- **OPEN:** All year, except 24 Dec-3 Jan
- **ROOMS:** 11 rooms: deluxe, superior, suite, single, twin
- **PRICE:** B&B - Single €185, Double €225, Deluxe €255

- **NOTES:**
Restaurant open 7am-10.30am, 12.30pm-3pm lunch and
6.30pm-11pm dinner all week (no lunch Sat). No wheelchair access. Street parking. Locked car parks nearby on
the Green. No facilities for children.

- **DIRECTIONS:**
30 mins driving from Dublin airport, 5 mins from Trinity
College, 1 min from Grafton Street.

THE CLARENCE

Robert van Eerde
6-8 Wellington Quay
Dublin 2
Tel: (01) 407 0800 Fax: 407 0820
reservations@theclarence.ie
www.theclarence.ie

The gorgeous Clarence has USPs – Unique Selling Points – to burn. Don't count 'em, just enjoy 'em.

Everyone in hospitality wants a USP – a Unique Selling Point – to separate them from the herd, to make them the destination that you are going to choose.

The only problem with The Clarence is that virtually every detail of the place is a USP. The design of the bedrooms and the public spaces? Unmatched by another hotel. The Guggi canvases that decorate the hotel? Superb, and remember that they hung them here years before Guggi began to fetch the big prices he now enjoys thanks to celebrity status. The style of their restaurant, The Tea Room? Superlative, and so romantic that this remains the city's great date restaurant. And Antony Ely's cooking in The Tea Room? Amongst the best – and most distinctive – in the city, not least the benchmark breakfasts which are as good as it gets.

That is one heck of a lot of USPs – that is a gaggle of USPs – and it explains why The Clarence is truly special, and unique. Yes it is pricey, and it is worth every cent.

● **OPEN:** All year
● **ROOMS:** 49 rooms, incl penthouse & suites
● **PRICE:** €315-€670 per person sharing

● **NOTES:**
All major credit cards accepted. Dinner from €55. Full wheelchair access. Valet parking. Children welcome, cots, toys, video games, children's meals.

● **DIRECTIONS:**
Overlooking the River Liffey, on the South side, approximately 150 metres up from the Ha'penny Bridge. 30-45 minutes' drive from Dublin airport.

MARBLE HALL

Shelagh Conway
81 Marlborough Road
Donnybrook, Dublin 4
Tel: (01) 497 7350
marblehall@eircom.net
www.marblehall.ie

Shelagh Conway's sumptuous, meticulous breakfasts are emblematic of the exacting standards of Marble Hall.

It must be in the blood. Shelagh Conway runs one of the best, most meticulously managed B&B's you can find anywhere in Ireland, and the fact that you can find it in Dublin – a city with a raft of overpriced and underperforming places to stay – makes MH even more special.

But the lineage thing must play its part, for if you took yourself over to the west coast, to Galway city, and stayed in the meticulous and marvellous Devon Dell B&B, then you would find yourself praising the fabulous standards and delicious cooking of Berna Kelly, who is none other than Ms Conway's sister. It's a family affair.

Both women understand everything about how to make a B&B a special place. Fabulous housekeeping, fabulous breakfasts – you won't get a better breakfast in Dublin than the one prepared by Shelagh at Marble Hall – and true, genuine hospitality all interact to make this some-place special, a place whose standards are a joy to enjoy. A decent society would erect a statue to these women.

- **OPEN:** All year
- **ROOMS:** Three rooms
- **PRICE:** B&B €50 per person sharing
- **CREDIT CARDS:** No credit cards accepted

- **NOTES:**
Not suitable for children. No wheelchair access. No dinner. Secure parking.

- **DIRECTIONS:**
Marlborough Road runs between Ranelagh and Donnybrook villages. Marble Hall is on the right hand side, near the top of the road, driving from Donnybrook.

MERRION HALL

54-56 Merrion Road
Ballsbridge
Dublin 4
Tel: (01) 668 1426
merrionhall@iol.ie
www.halpinsprivatehotels.com

Brilliant service from Can-Do! staff is the trademark of Pat Halpin's Dublin houses, making for great retreats from the stresses of work and travel.

'Sure, solid and safe bets.' That's what Pat Halpin's Dublin houses offer to the traveller and, in a city where standards often incline to the unreliable and unremarkable, Mr Halpin's achievement is considerable.

Aberdeen Lodge, also featured in this book, is another of his safe houses, and Merrion Hall shares its trademark of superb service and a conspiracy to shield you from the stresses and strains of business and travel. To put it quite simply: these are Can-Do! people, friendly without being interfering, focused on your needs, balancing intimacy and anonymity, people who make you glad you have arrived. Others first off ask for your credit card number: in Merrion they offer tea, newspapers, helpful information, and they remain focused on you until you leave. The rooms are restful thanks to the use of neutral colours, the housekeeping is meticulous – another Halpin trademark – and Merrion works as a reliable and restorative address, close enough to the city, just far enough away.

● **OPEN:** All year
● **ROOMS:** 28 rooms, including eight suites
● **PRICE:** €65-€90 per person sharing, €99-€120 single, suite supplement €50

● **NOTES:**
Light 'drawing room' menu, €8-€15 per course, extensive wine list. Secure parking. Wheelchair access. Children - not suitable for children under 7yrs.

● **DIRECTIONS:**
Ballsbridge is located south of the city centre and Merrion Hall is just opposite the Four Seasons Hotel.

THE MORRISON

Anthony Kenna
Ormond Quay
Dublin 1
Tel: (01) 887 2400, Fax: 874 4039
info@morrisonhotel.ie
www.morrisonhotel.ie

The Morrison is super-
trendy, but first off it is a
rock-solid, professional,
brilliantly run city hotel.

Our kids love The Morrison. 'So what?' says you. 'What
sort of critical assessment is that?'

Well, the strange thing about children's take on a different address is this: if they don't feel immediately comfortable in a place, they respond instantly and instinctive-
ly: they simply don't want to walk into the room. This has
happened to us before, trying to coax them into some
hotel or country house and then having to live with the
fact that they refuse to accept what they know feels
wrong about a room, about a public space.

So, the fact that they reckon The Morrison is hunky-dory
tells you more about the successful aesthetic of this place
than any amount of talk about its groovy clientele, or its
high-profile designer, or any of that hype. The Morrison is
simply comfortable, charming, welcoming, tactile, a beautifully conceived hotel, with excellent staff and – right
now – some of the finest cooking to be enjoyed in the
city. So, bring the children, or at least the inner child.

● **OPEN:** All year, except 25-26 Dec
● **ROOMS:** 90 rooms and suites, incl penthouse
● **PRICE:** From €270-€310 per room. Supplements
apply for suites and superior rooms.

● **NOTES:**
All major cards accepted. Wheelchair access. Children
welcome. Parking rate offered in Jervis St Car Park.
Halo Restaurant and Cafe Bar open daily. Lobo, late
night club open till 3am. Lunch €28, Dinner €65.

● **DIRECTIONS:**
On the north side of the river, near the Millennium Bridge.

THE RED BANK LODGE

Terry McCoy
5-7 Church Street, Skerries
County Dublin
Tel: (01) 849 1005, Fax: 849 1598
redbank@eircom.net
www.redbank.ie

Some of the best fish cookery you will find is Terry McCoy's secret in The Red Bank: book a room and make the most of a trip north to Skerries.

Others of his generation of chefs and hoteliers have begun to put away the knives and head off for the golf course and the g'n't at noon, but Terry McCoy not only shows no signs of giving up, he shows no signs of slowing up.

His Red Bank restaurant remains a north Dublin destination thanks to some seriously fine fish cookery, and his development in the last few years of no fewer than 18 rooms for guests shows that young blood courses in this guy's veins. The rooms are as professionally accomplished as everything else in this slick operation, quietly comfortable, with an ageless style that matches McCoy's own youthful métier. This isn't bling bling territory: this is an older, graceful, subtle style of comfort and decoration that suits the style of this venerable restaurant. So, get away from the madding crowd for the night, book a room and enjoy fine cooking and hospitality 'oop northside.

● **OPEN:** All year
● **ROOMS:** 18 rooms, all en suite
● **PRICE:** From €60 per person sharing

● **NOTES:**
All major cards accepted. Restaurant open for dinner and Sunday lunch. Special offer, €90 dinner B&B. On street parking. Children under 5 free. Wheelchair access.

● **DIRECTIONS:**
Skerries is 29km north of the centre of Dublin, and 20 minutes' drive north from Dublin airport. The guesthouse is on the sea front.

BALLYNAHINCH CASTLE

Patrick O'Flaherty
Ballinafad, Recess, Connemara
County Galway
Tel & Fax: (095) 31006
bhinch@iol.ie
www.ballynahinch-castle.com

A beacon of genuine, democratic hospitality, Ballynahinch is one of the best addresses.

There are certain addresses that exemplify the Irish zeitgeist of hospitality at its zenith, and Ballynahinch is one of the foremost examples.

Patrick O'Flaherty and his superb team do what they do in a way that no other nationality of innkeeper could achieve. Their relaxed yet efficient way of cooking and caring, of maintaining and mastering, of offering hospitality and cooking, is uniquely Irish. It has a strong element of understatement, a modesty that belies the grandness of this big castle. It has a strong historical continuum which the modern hotel respects and acknowledges. It is a place where rich and not-so-rich, young and old, all feel comfortable, oh-so-comfortable. As such, the work of Mr O'Flaherty and his team has a democratic spirit to it: Ballynahinch works because it is genuinely open to all, and all who come here are treated equally, are treated as well as the team can manage, and they manage that superbly. Ballynahinch is a beacon in Irish hospitality: don't miss it.

● **OPEN:** All year, except Feb
● **ROOMS:** 40 rooms, including three suites
● **PRICE:** €85-€197 per person sharing, single supplement €27

● **NOTES:**
All major cards accepted. Dinner in restaurant, €45. Full wheelchair access. Children welcome.

● **DIRECTIONS:**
From Galway, look out for signs for Clifden (N59). Pass through Moycullen, Oughterard, then Maam Cross, then Recess, and you will begin to see their signs.

DELPHI LODGE

Peter Mantle
Leenane, Connemara
County Galway
Tel: (095) 42222 Fax: (095) 42296
delfish@iol.ie
www.delphilodge.ie

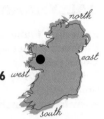

Is there a more awe-inspiring location for a house than that enjoyed by Delphi Lodge? We don't think so, and everything else here is just as fine.

Dephi Lodge brings it all together. Good company, great cooking, and a spectacular location – hell, spectacular isn't in it: Delphi's location is awesomely gorgeous, set as it is amidst the stern splendour of the Leenane valley. To drive into this part of Galway from the north, heading down the N59 into the Connemara Gateway, you can witness the awesome embrace of the Partry Mountains lit by a William Blake sky (excuse the hyperbole, but that's what we scribbled in our notebook last time we did the route). Who needs mind-expanding pharmaceuticals when Mother Nature drops this on you?

And arriving at Delphi, then, is like arriving at your dream destination, the lake stretching out from the front of the house, some good fishin' and huntin' to be had if that's your bag, whilst food lovers wait to see just what delights chef Cliodna O'Donogue has cooked up for the table that evening. Great wines from a great cellar, excellent convivial company, and an all-round civilised place.

● **OPEN:** Mid Jan-mid Dec
● **ROOMS:** 12 rooms, all en suite (seven with lake view)
● **PRICE:** €65 standard, €125 lake view per person sharing

● **NOTES:**
Visa & Mastercard. Dinner at 8pm, communal €48. Limited wheelchair access. Secure parking. Young children discouraged.

● **DIRECTIONS:**
8 miles northwest of Leenane on the Louisburgh road. In woods on left about half mile after the Mountain Spa.

DEVON DELL

Berna Kelly
47 Devon Park
Lower Salthill, Galway city
Tel: (091) 528306
devondell@iol.ie
www.devondell.com

Devon Dell is just where you want to be on a Galway visit, being looked after by Berna Kelly.

It must be in the blood. Berna Kelly is one of the great B&B keepers, and so is her sister, Shelagh, who runs the superlative Marble Hall, in Dublin's Donnybrook. From west coast to east coast, the sisters have it sorted and, best of all, have you sorted.

Mrs Kelly's manner is all care and concern, hard work, attention to detail, all of it founded in an utterly true hospitality that gladdens the heart. Hospitality this instinctive is a joy, and allied to such a high level of perfection when it comes to preparing her rooms and cooking breakfasts, it makes for a combination that just can't be beat. You feel mothered, you feel taken care of and – suddenly – you don't have a care in the world. You are having the great time in Galway. The house is small, prim, pretty, decorated with good, timeless taste. The choice at breakfast is as staggering as the care and attention lavished on every manner of breakfast treat from French toast to kippers, poached plums to apple and nut waffle with maple syrup.

- **OPEN:** Feb-Oct
- **ROOMS:** 2 double rooms, 1 twin & 1 single, en suite
- **PRICE:** €35-€40 per person sharing

- **NOTES:**
No credit cards. No meals. No smoking house. No wheelchair access. Secure parking. No facilities for children.

- **DIRECTIONS:**
Find Fr Griffin Rd, and follow to T-junction, where you take left into Lr Salthill rd. After approx 500m, having passed two pubs, take first right. Go 100m to fork in road, take left and very sharp left into cul-de-sac.

DOLPHIN BEACH

**The Foyle family
Lower Sky Road, Clifden
Connemara, County Galway
Tel: (095) 21204 Fax: 22935
dolphinbeach@iol.free.ie
connemara.net/dolphinbeachhouse**

Dolphin Beach has gone from new arrival to cult destination in double-quick time. Visit this ace house and you'll see why.

No other address has moved from newly opened to cult destination as speedily as Billy and Barbara Folye's Dolphin Beach. And it's no wonder, for this is one of those houses that simply does the magic, a place that has serenity, sophistication, glamour and good times running as its zeitgeist. In the crowded world and stratospheric standards of Connemara accommodation, Dolphin Beach had to be good to prosper, but it has turned out to be more than good.

The bedrooms, in particular, have a gracious simplicity that is irresistible, and whilst they are glam enough to be in the design magazines, they aren't prissy or self-conscious. And the public rooms have that spaciousness and grace that means you simply want to turn up and chill out. The Foyle girls run the place with great charm, with Sinead in charge of the kitchen, from which you can expect good shellfish, good salads, good country cooking for main courses, fine puds and good wines. Cult indeed.

● **OPEN:** Feb-1 Dec
● **ROOMS:** Nine rooms, all en suite
● **PRICE:** €65-€80 per person sharing. Single supplement €20

● **NOTES:**
Dinner 7pm, €37. Enclosed parking. Children over 12 welcome. Wheelchair access.

● **DIRECTIONS:**
Take the Sky road out of Clifden, take the lower fork for 1 mile. It's the house on the sea side. Clifden is approximately 1 hour's drive from Galway.

FERMOYLE LODGE

Nicola Stronach & J-P Maire
Costello, Connemara
County Galway
Tel: (091) 786111 Fax: 786154
fermoylelodge@eircom.net
www.fermoylelodge.com

Fermoyle Lodge is one of the glorious houses of Connemara. Mysterious, isolated, magical, luxurious, it's a Heathcliffian melodrama all by itself.

Nicola Stronach and JP Maire know how to do things right. That is immediately evident when you first see and walk into Fermoyle, after the fun of the higgledy-piggledy drive through the bog to finally discover the house in its fabulous isolation, for this is a glorious house, a classic of its type. And Nicola and JP have done full design justice to this masterpiece, originally built by the Berridge family and finished in 1875. Understated, demure, just right, appropriate, these are the sort of adjectives that come tripping off the tongue as you tour the rooms, rooms where comfort is underscored with a quiet luxuriousness that is completely winning.

But JP also knows how to take care of the culinary side of things, using McGeough's superb butcher's shop to source his meat, getting fresh fish from Flemings, sourcing excellent wines, and thereby offering the real tastes of Connemara. Just make sure, when booking, that you give yourself enough days to enjoy this really special retreat.

- **OPEN:** Apr-Oct
- **ROOMS:** six rooms, all with private bathrooms
- **PRICE:** B&B €85 per person sharing

- **NOTES:**
Visa, Mastercard. Dinner €40, 7.30pm, 24 hours' notice required (any special diets should be mentioned when booking). No wheelchair access. Secure parking. Not suitable for young children.

- **DIRECTIONS:**
From Oughterard, turn left before bridge at The Bridge Restaurant. Lodge is 10 miles from Oughterard on right.

GALWAY HARBOUR HOTEL

Sinead O'Reilly
New Dock Road
Galway, County Galway
Tel: (091) 569466 Fax: 569455
stay@harbour.ie
www.galwayharbourhotel.com

Great value for money and a great dockside location close to town make the Harbour Hotel a great choice for a wild Galway city weekend away.

Galway city's radical development has seen the creation of many new hotels, from budget boxes all the way up to the stylish and expensive Radisson. The Harbour Hotel strikes a nice balance somewhere in between these two: value for money is very keen, the staff at check-in are welcoming and professional, there is free car parking so you can evade the clampers, it takes only two minutes to walk into town, and the bedrooms are very good indeed; spacious, painted in soothing, neutral modern colours, with big bathrooms that sadly suffer from overly loud extractor fans. Little touches such as CD players are more than one expects in this price range, and show the smart thinking behind the Harbour Hotel.

The formula has been very successful, and so there are plans to add a leisure centre and to up the spec. We would think it more important to concentrate on curing the weakness that is their breakfast offer, but what do we know? But, for value and location, HH is hard to beat.

● **OPEN:** All year
● **ROOMS:** 96 rooms, including those with harbour view, and executive rooms
● **PRICE:** €59-€89 per person sharing, €92 single. Upgrades apply for superior rooms.

● **NOTES:**
All major credit cards accepted. Restaurant and bar serve lunch, dinner and snacks. Complimentary secure parking. Conference facilities. Children welcome.

● **DIRECTIONS:**
Follow signs to the harbour, the hotel is on your left.

GARRAUNBAUN HOUSE

John & Catherine Finnegan
Moyard
Connemara
County Galway
Tel: (095) 41649 Fax: 41649
garraunbaun.house@ireland.com

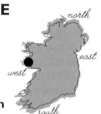

A super-comfortable Victorian house that offers some of the best views you will find in Connemara, Garraunbaun House is a dream place to escape to.

Garraunbaun is one of those houses that really does have it all. It is pretty as a picture, a classic Victorian country mansion dating from 1850, but built and decorated in such a smart, timeless style that every aspect of this pretty place seems utterly contemporary.

It is a comfortable house, with comfortable public rooms that invite you to sit down and chill out. From the bedrooms, with their gargantuan spaces and huge beds, you can peer out at the Twelve Bens, a view that is amongst the most breathtaking you can enjoy in Ireland. This is Connemara triumphant: wild, unspoilt, severe, poetic, capacious, magnificent.

Delia Finnegan's good country cooking completes the equation of a feel-good address. Dinners are the work of a smart, motivated cook with a real zest for the challenge of the kitchen and the knowledge of just how to get the best out of her local foods. Put yourself into this fine house and with this food, and it's Connemara incarnate.

- **OPEN:** All year
- **ROOMS:** Four rooms, all with private bathroom
- **PRICE:** €45-€70 per person

- **NOTES:**
Dinner, 8pm, €30, separate or communal tables. No wheelchair access. Enclosed car park. Children welcome, high chair, cot, babysitting, video films for all ages.

- **DIRECTIONS:**
From Galway take the Clifden rd, from Clifden take the Westport rd, and 9 miles further the Garraunbaun sign is on left hand side.

IVERNA COTTAGE

Patricia & William Farrell
Salahoona, Spiddal
County Galway
Tel: (091) 553762
ivernacottage@ireland.com
www.ivernacottage.8m.com

Iverna Cottage offers hospitality that is nothing less than a therapeutic pleasure. Check in and check out the sublime cooking and hospitality.

Patricia and William Farrell's Iverna has the magic. In the morass of undistinguished – and frankly frequently pretentious – housing that trails from Galway to Spiddal, their stone house is demure, pretty, much cared for.

Walk inside, then, and you are in the land of books, candlelight, scents, culture, with maybe a glass of wine to share with the hosts. It is such a relaxing place you feel you have moved miles from the main road to Galway, but there it is, still outside. Forget it: you are already someplace else.

'I don't write a breakfast menu, but people can have whatever they want, and they usually have everything!' says Mrs Farrell. So, start with some fruit, then some cereals, then a grand fry-up, or maybe kippers, or poached eggs with spinach. 'One of the best breakfasts I've had in any B&B', says our mate Declan, a man who knows. The breakfast is as meticulously conceived and executed as the housekeeping and the hospitality: someplace special.

- **OPEN:** May-mid Sept
- **ROOMS:** Four rooms
- **PRICE:** €35-€40 per person sharing. Single €50-€60.

- **NOTES:**
No specified wheelchair access, though a number of wheelchair users have happily negotiated the step into the house. Children welcome, 33% discount, 2 family rooms. No dinner. No credit cards.

- **DIRECTIONS:**
The house is exactly one mile west of Spiddal on the coast road.

KILMURVEY HOUSE

Treasa & Bertie Joyce
Kilmurvey Bay, Inis Mor
Aran Islands, County Galway
Tel: (099) 61218 Fax: (099) 61397
kilmurveyhouse@eircom.net
www.kilmurveyhouse.com

Put beautiful Kilmurvey Bay together
with beautiful Kilmurvey House and
you have the perfect Aran Island
recipe for the best times imaginable.

Kilmurvey Bay is one of our favourite places to go swimming in Ireland, the sea crystal-clear, the sand mother-of-pearl white, the graceful arc of the beach like some undiscovered Mediterranean secret. Such bliss!

What a boon to the traveller, then, that Treasa Joyce's distinguished house should be set so close to Kilmurvey Bay, and the pair of them not much more than a few minutes' jaunt by bus up the road from Kilronan.

If Kilmurvey Bay is the Aran Island beach of your dreams, then Kilmurvey House is the Aran Island B&B of your dreams. Mrs Joyce specialises in great housekeeping – hang on, make that superlative housekeeping – great domestic cooking with bumper breakfasts – not too much, you're going swimming! – and lovely, comforting dinners for when you get back, sun-scorched, exhausted – and the result is that you are very quickly going to feel like that cat who got the cream. Such great hospitality and such elemental beauty means taking your leave isn't easy.

- **OPEN:** 1 Apr-16 Oct
- **ROOMS:** 12 rooms, all en suite (seven family rooms)
- **PRICE:** €35-€42 per person sharing. Single €50-€60

- **NOTES:**
Dinner €25, 7pm, please book in advance.
No wheelchair access. Children welcome.

- **DIRECTIONS:**
Take boat from Rosaveel in Connemara. When you arrive in Kilronan, the house is a further 7km from the ferry port. On arrival, take one of the tour buses that crowd down at the port.

NORMAN VILLA

Mark & Dee Keogh
86 Lower Salthill
Galway city
Tel & Fax: (091) 521131
normanvilla@oceanfree.net
www.normanvilla.com

Mark and Dee Keogh collect art, and make art: their subject is their wonderful Norman Villa.

Mark and Dee Keogh are avid collectors of contemporary Irish art, as any visitor to the beautiful Norman Villa will appreciate from the moment they walk through the door.

But the Keoghs are not just collectors; they are artists themselves, and their canvas is their extraordinary house. They play with space and colour, they play with volume and simplicity, they range from the sense of attack of Fontana to the calmness of McSweeney, from the formalism of Moholy-Nagy to the energy of Yeats. But no artist has spent a comparable amount of time on a single work as the time spent by Mark and Dee on their beloved Norman. Their endless permutations with furniture, with paintings, with re-arranging bedrooms, can be compared only to a painter working away, working away, on a piece of art. The result is a house that is outstanding in its success as a place to stay, a place to relax. And, finally, they are masters of the greatest art form of all: hospitality.

● **OPEN:** Mar-31 Oct
● **ROOMS:** Four double rooms, two family rooms
● **PRICE:** €50-€55 per person sharing for room and continental breakfast. €65-€70 single.

● **NOTES:**
No dinner (plenty of local restaurants). No wheelchair access. Secure parking. No facilities for children under 12.

● **DIRECTIONS:**
Follow signs to Salthill, then to Lower Salthill. House is next door to PJ Flahertys pub, 15 minutes to the city centre.

THE QUAY HOUSE

**Paddy & Julie Foyle
Beach Road, Clifden
Connemara, County Galway
Tel: (095) 21369 Fax: 21608
thequay@iol.ie
www.thequayhouse.com**

Paddy and Julia Foyle do everything from design to hospitality to cooking in their own inimitable way.

Being such a celebrated pair on account of their impeccable sense of style has tended to take focus away from the fact that Paddy and Julia Foyle are also amongst the most hospitable people on the planet.

Indeed, along with being supreme arbiters of interior design, as they demonstrate in the extraordinary Quay House, they are supreme arbiters of a true Irish welcome, of the ability to make people feel right at home. And, this ability starts right at the very beginning; we have seen Paddy Foyle chat to people on the telephone after they have rung to make a booking, and within minutes Mr Foyle has them chattering away as if they have known the man and his family all their lives. It's a great skill, and it is spontaneous, genuine, and infinitely generous.

Stylists, hosts, and don't overlook that they are also great cooks, so eating in Quay House brings the triumvirate of temptations to a soaring crescendo. There is nowhere else which is remotely like Quay House: a place apart.

● **OPEN:** Mid Mar-Early-Nov
● **ROOMS:** 14 en suite rooms, including rooms with kitchens
● **PRICE:** €140 per room, B&B, €25 single supplement

● **NOTES:**
Visa, Mastercard. No dinner, but snacks on request, and plenty of local restaurants. Full wheelchair access. Street parking. Children welcomed and encouraged.

● **DIRECTIONS:**
Take the N59 from Galway to Clifden. The Quay House is down on the quays, overlooking the harbour.

RENVYLE

Ronnie Counihan
Letterfrack, Connemara
County Galway
Tel: (095) 43571 Fax: 43515
renvyle@iol.ie
www.renvyle.com

Constant improvements on every front show that Renvyle is a progressive place, but nothing alters the calm charm of the staff and the good food.

Tim O'Sullivan's cooking won him the first prize in the annual Moreau Chablis fish cookery competition in 2003, fending off such super-star cooks as Raymond McArdle, David Foley and Martina O'Donovan. Mr O'Sullivan's commitment in the kitchen is echoed in the stylish Renvyle by manager Ronnie Counihan's commitment to driving this long-established destination – Renvyle opened its doors in 1883! – forwards.

Improvements are constant – new suites were added in 2003 along with refurbishment of many other bedrooms – and whilst this is admirable, what is even better about Renvyle is the fact that its verities remain constant: super-friendly staff, a genuine welcome, a complete lack of pretension, and some seriously good food to be enjoyed whilst a fine pianist tinkles away in the lovely dining room. These standards and consistencies mean that Renvyle is one of the best chill-out zones imaginable, and it is always a pleasure to be stepping into that fine lobby once more.

● **OPEN:** Feb-Dec
● **ROOMS:** 68 rooms
● **PRICE:** €46-€96 per person sharing. Single supplement €20.50. Look out for frequent offers (see website).

● **NOTES:**
All major cards accepted. Restaurant, serving dinner 7pm-9.30pm, €40. Children welcome, many facilities. Full wheelchair access.

● **DIRECTIONS:**
The hotel is signposted from Kylemore. At Letterfrack, turn right, and travel four miles to hotel gates.

SEA MIST HOUSE

Sheila Griffin
Clifden, Connemara
County Galway
Tel: (095) 21441
sgriffin@eircom.net
www.connemara.net/seaview

Sea Mist is one of the most charming, vivacious B&Bs you can find, a place packed with people having a ball.

Sheila Griffin has created one of the most charming B&B's you can find in Ireland, and what makes Sea Mist even more special is to find such a gem in a commercial tourist town such as Clifden. And, whilst the house is almost in the centre of town, it feels miles apart from the crowds. The motivation of this sweet house is dedicated to care and concern for guests' well-being, and to this end Ms Griffin has arranged the house and its furnishings with the careful eye of the painter she is. It is an aesthetic treat to be here, to enjoy the tactility, simplicity and sensuality of the rooms, to be in the colourful, giddy embrace of the breakfast room on a fine morning, enjoying local butcher Des Moran's smashing pork sausages – do not miss these fab sausages – and his equally excellent white pudding, enjoying some duck eggs with feta, enjoying just being here, in the company of so many people having a really great time. Sea Mist is consummately relaxing, a truly great destination in clamorous, glamorous Connemara.

● **OPEN:** All year, except Christmas
● **ROOMS:** Six rooms, all en suite
● **PRICE:** €35-€45 per person sharing, single supplement €15-€20

● **NOTES:**
Visa, Mastercard. No dinner. No wheelchair access. No facilities for children. Limited enclosed parking.

● **DIRECTIONS:**
Right beside the Bank of Ireland in the centre of Clifden. Clifden is approximately 1 hour's drive from Galway city.

ALLO'S TOWNHOUSE

Helen Mullane
41 Church Street
Listowel
County Kerry
Tel: (068) 22880 Fax: 22803
www.allos.ie

Lovely rooms that show real design flair, one of the prettiest bars in the country and a relaxed bistro is the triple-play in Helen Mullane's house.

There is real design flair, real style originality, in the three rooms that comprise Helen Mullane's narrow old townhouse in pretty Listowel.

The style has the same grace and favour as that shown in the lovely bar – for our money, one of the most beautiful and authentic bars in the country – with objects chosen with great care and then put in just the right place, making for great feng shui and, consequently, a feeling of great restfulness. The bathrooms, in particular, are superbly accomplished.

And Theo Lynch's cooking in both the bar and the bistro is bang on target: lovely comfort food executed with considerable flair and passion. Here is a cook who makes classic Irish dishes, such as bacon and cabbage, or fried fish with potatoes, seem newly minted. Great service from local girls and superb value for money mean nowhere else in Listowel gets a look in. At present Ms Mullane is offering a room only rate that is super value for money.

● **OPEN:** All year. Closed Sun & Mon
● **ROOMS:** Three rooms, all en suite
● **PRICE:** €40 per person sharing. Room only - no breakfast available. Single supplement €10

● **NOTES:**
Dinner and bar food served in Allo's Bar & Bistro.
No wheelchair access. Children welcome.

● **DIRECTIONS:**
1 hour's drive from Limerick on the N69. Allo's Townhouse is in the centre of Listowel, on the one-way system. You will find it opposite the main Garda station.

THE CAPTAIN'S HOUSE

Jim & Mary Milhench
The Mall, Dingle
County Kerry
Tel: (066) 915 1531 Fax: 915 1079
captigh@eircom.net
homepage.eircom.net/~captigh/

Just watch the speedy, svelte and unobtrusive way in which Mary Milhench assembles a welcoming tray of good things for guests: it's magic.

Hospitality is an instinct with Mary Milhench. There she is, welcoming you in, sorting you out, chatting away about what you have been up to, and all the while she is making the coffee, slicing some fruit loaf, lathering jam and cream onto scones and, suddenly, hey presto! there is a delicious welcoming treat of a tray of food in front of you before you even know it. What a girl!

Along with Jim Milhench, Mary powers this tiny, intimate house along on a wave of fabulous energy. The house-keeping is superb, the breakfasts sublime, the welcome 24 carat. It's a little prize of a place, a house that Dingle regulars return to time after time, usually requesting the room they stayed in on their last visit. Mr Milhench, by the by, even finds time to run a garden shop, so the horticulturally inclined amongst you should pay a visit there too, and do ask about Jim's tempura of bay leaf. The Milhenchs are also wise guides to the newest restaurant openings in this busy town, so you will be sorted from A to Z. Fab.

- **OPEN:** 15 Mar-15 Nov
- **ROOMS:** Eight rooms, one suite, all en suite
- **PRICE:** €45-€50 per person sharing. Single rate €55. Suite €60 per person sharing

- **NOTES:**
Visa, Mastercard accepted. No meals. No smoking house. No wheelchair access. No facilities for children.

- **DIRECTIONS:**
Follow signs to Dingle town centre. The Captain's House is 200m on the left, after the first big round-about.

CARRIG HOUSE

Frank & Mary Slattery
Caragh Lake, Killorglin
County Kerry
Tel: (066) 976 9100 Fax: 976 9166
info@carrighouse.com
www.carrighouse.com

A fantastic location, great cooking and hospitality make Carrig a don't-miss! on the Ring of Kerry.

Aeons ago, we stayed at Carrig House, at a time before Frank and Mary Slattery took over this fine, lakeside house. The unremitting misery of the experience remains with us still: the greyness of the house; the greyness of the hospitality; the greyness of what was regarded as acceptable in food and service back in the 1980's in Ireland.

Today, thanks to the Slatterys, the experience at Carrig House is pristine, polished, international, and yet wholly Irish. This fine house chimes with a true hospitality, is both relaxing and reviving, the cooking is excellent, and Carrig offers a magical country house experience that captures the essence of being on the Ring of Kerry.

The cooking has real flair, in dishes such as a Lyonnaise salad of grilled kippers and sautéed chicken livers, or some fine roast smoked pork from Cork city, and desserts will persuade you to reach for some pudding wine. At breakfast, eggs are scrambled to benchmark status. The music isn't quite right, but everything else sure is.

- **OPEN:** 1 Mar-1 Dec
- **ROOMS:** 16 rooms (including two suites)
- **PRICE:** B&B from €75 per person sharing. Single supplement in double room, €45.

- **NOTES:**
Visa, Master, Diners accepted. Wheelchair access. Children over 8yrs only. Dinner from 6.30pm, €40-€45 per person.

- **DIRECTIONS:**
From Killorglin, take N70, direction Glenbeigh. After 2.5 miles turn left for Caragh Lake, then 1.5miles turn right at School. The entrance is half a mile further on the left.

10 PLACES WITH
GREAT BATHROOMS

1

BALLYVOLANE HOUSE
FERMOY, Co CORK

2

BARNABROW HOUSE
CLOYNE, Co CORK

3

CASTLE LESLIE
GLASLOUGH, Co MONAGHAN

4

COAST TOWNHOUSE
TRAMORE, Co WATERFORD

5

EMLAGH HOUSE
DINGLE, Co KERRY

6

HILTON PARK
CLONES, Co MONAGHAN

7

LONGUEVILLE HOUSE
MALLOW, Co CORK

8

MOY HOUSE
LAHINCH, Co CLARE

9

THE MUSTARD SEED
BALLINGARRY, Co LIMERICK

10

SHELBURNE LODGE
KENMARE, Co KERRY

EMLAGH HOUSE

Michael & Marion Kavanagh
Dingle
County Kerry
Tel: (066) 915 2345 Fax: 915 2369
info@emlaghhouse.com
www.emlaghhouse.com

In Emlagh, everything is the best it can be, and every detail is constantly examined to see how it can be made better: a truly inspiring house.

The meticulous attention paid by Marion and Grainne Kavanagh to every single facet and detail of Emlagh House is an inspiration. The duvets are the best. The crockery is the best. The tea strainers, for goodness' sake! are the best. The power showers are the best – and indeed these are awesomely powerful, so prepare to be blasted out of your lazy Dingle hangover.

The CD players in the rooms are superlative Bose, and they even have a stash of CDs you can choose from. Breakfast offers superb treats such as baked eggs with ham and cream and a little light cheese topping, but you have to work hard to drag your gaze away from the glorious views out across the sea. The paintings and etchings they have hung by Kerry painters are glorious, and whilst the house is indeed grand, it never feels indulgent or precious. Instead, it feels like someplace special, a house where the evident luxury really does make you feel good. And so, whilst Emlagh is expensive, it is well, well worth it.

- **OPEN:** mid Feb-end Nov
- **ROOMS:** 10 rooms
- **PRICE:** B&B €75-120 per person sharing, €40 single supplement

- **NOTES:**
Visa, Master. Evening meals available. One room fully wheelchair accessible. Private car park. Children under eight years not encouraged.

- **DIRECTIONS:**
As one drives West towards Dingle, Emlagh House is the first turn left at the entrance to the town.

HAWTHORN HOUSE

Noel & Mary O'Brien
Shelbourne Street, Kenmare
County Kerry
Tel: (064) 41035 Fax: 41932
info@hawthornhousekenmare.con
www.hawthornhousekenmare.con

Kenmare is full of distinguished addresses, and Mary O'Brien's Hawthorn House is yet another one of them, a smashing, cosy, fun house.

Amiable, unpretentious, friendly, fun: what a pleasure to be back in Mary O'Brien's spick and span B&B, right in the heart of pretty Kenmare, Ireland's gastronomic heart.

Mrs O'Brien greets one and all as if they were old friends, and indeed when you stay here, one is struck by just how many regulars the house has. For newcomers, the sense of relaxation, of genuine hospitality, of having your wishes taken care of even before you express them, is just some sort of bliss.

At breakfast-time, the decibel level is already at full pitch, as everyone enjoys super cooking – lovely poached eggs, nice brown bread, good tea and coffee – and another fine day beckons. The craic has already begun, and it is only 8am!

The air of relaxed comfort that pervades this simple house is always a true treat, and Hawthorn is a model B&B. Everyone loves it, everyone comes back, and it stands alongside all the other great addresses in Kenmare.

- **OPEN:** All year, except Christmas
- **ROOMS:** Eight rooms, en suite
- **PRICE:** €40-€45 per person sharing, Single €50

- **NOTES:**
Visa and Mastercard accepted. No dinner. No wheelchair access. Enclosed private parking. Children welcome, babysitting available.

- **DIRECTIONS:**
There are three main streets in Kenmare. Hawthorn House is situated on Shelbourne Street, the quietest of the three.

ISKEROON

Geraldine Burkitt & David Hare
Bunavalla, Caherdaniel
County Kerry
Tel: (066) 947 5119 Fax: 947 5488
info@iskeroon.com
www.iskeroon.com

The wildest most romantic location, and the most imaginative design makes Iskeroon a true peach.

We pointed out the following earlier in the year, but it is an achievement of such staggering proportions, and it is so little noted by the mainstream media, that it really does bear repeating.

In 'The Hotel Book: Great Escapes Europe', the gorgeous Iskeroon is the only Irish address to be included, up there in the pack with such global bling-bling brands as Sweden's Ice Hotel or Reid's Palace in Madeira.

This is some achievement, but there is even more to consider. For Iskeroon, in all its design glory and in its extraordinary location, a location almost beyond description, is not a self-conscious place, not at all. It's a quiet, peaceful, mature, sophisticated house. No glitz, and the glam is true and modest, and David and Geraldine run the house with good grace and quiet efficiency, ministering to its needs – Iskeroon is one of those houses that you begin to talk about as if it was a character itself, like Galway's Norman Villa. It's remarkable, and unforgettable.

● **OPEN:** 1 May-30 Sep
● **ROOMS:** Three rooms, each with private bathroom. Self-catering apartment for two
● **PRICE:** €60 per person sharing. Single supplement €25

● **NOTES:**
Visa, Mastercard accepted. Light supper available Mon-Fri, if pre booked, 8pm, €25. No wheelchairs. No children.

● **DIRECTIONS:**
Find the Scarriff Inn between Waterville and Caherdaniel. Take sign to Bunavalla Pier. At the pier, go through gate marked 'private road', beside beach through pillars.

THE KILLARNEY PARK HOTEL

Padraig & Janet Treacy
Kenmare Place, Killarney
County Kerry
Tel: (064) 35555 Fax: 35266
info@killarneyparkhotel.ie
www.killarneyparkhotel.ie

Janet and Padraig Treacy
are amongst the most dis-
tinguished hoteliers and the
KP is their fab King Pin.

Every so often, after some dire experience in an Irish hotel – don't ask us about those places in Clare and Galway this year – we ask ourselves why Irish hoteliers don't make it their business to head down to Janet and Padraig Treacy's pair of Killarney hotels – in addition to the KP they also run the Ross Hotel in the town – and see for themselves and study for themselves how to run a hotel to the highest international standards.

For that is what manager Donagh Davern and his team achieve at the KP: the highest standards of hospitality and cooking. The KP is the King Pin of Irish hotels; it runs like a dream, powered by the most motivated staff we have ever encountered. The style, the cooking and the service are sublime, and with eight new treatment rooms added to the spa, the hotel is even more of a chill-out zone than before. Mr and Mrs Treacy are amongst the most distinguished hoteliers in the country. They should be in charge of our national tourism education: of course, they aren't.

- **OPEN:** All year, except Christmas
- **ROOMS:** 71 rooms
- **PRICE:** €250-€370 per room, €350-€720 suites

- **NOTES:**
Visa, Mastercard, Amex, Laser. Restaurant & Bar open daily, Dinner €52.50. Children welcome, babysitting and facilities available on request. Full wheelchair access.

- **DIRECTIONS:**
At 1st roundabout in Killarney (coming from Cork), take 1st exit for town centre. At 2nd roundabout take 2nd exit and at 3rd roundabout take 1st exit.

THE PARK HOTEL

Francis & John Brennan
Kenmare
County Kerry
Tel: (064) 41200 Fax: 41402
info@parkkenmare.com
www.parkkenmare.com

Francis Brennan is once again raising the bar with the opening of the new state-of-the-art Samas spa.

Late one evening in Kenmare, we brought our children into the Park for a cup of hot chocolate before bedtime. The staff were charming, witty, gracious, and the presentation of the chocolate for the kids – which came with some bumper petits fours – was nothing less than the art of service in action. The kids loved it.

That's what we love about the Park: it's art in action. The dedication of Francis Brennan and his team to achieving the highest standard runs right throughout this grand enterprise, from hot chocolate to the design spec for Samas, their brand new spa, which is set behind the hotel and which will occupy no less than 10,000 square feet of treatment rooms, pools and every bit of state-of-the-art spa accoutrement you can get. It's an ambitious step, a sign that Mr Brennan is aiming once again to break the mould, to raise expectations and to raise the bar, just as he has done with the standards set over the years by his luminary hotel. Even the hot chocolate is a star turn here.

- **OPEN:** 18 Apr-30 Nov & 23 Dec-2 Jan
- **ROOMS:** 46 rooms
- **PRICE:** €366 per person sharing, B&B

- **NOTES:**
All major cards accepted. Restaurant open daily, Dinner from 7pm, €64. Full wheelchair access. Secure parking. Private dining if required. Restaurant available to 8pm for under 6 year olds. Spa opens this year.

- **DIRECTIONS:**
At the top of Kenmare town.

PARKNASILLA

Jim Feeney
Sneem
County Kerry
Tel: (064) 45122, Fax: 45323
res@parknasilla-gsh.com
www.greatsouthernhotels.com

north
east
west
south

It's hard to resist the temptation, driving past Parknasilla, not to turn off the road, check into this lovely hotel, and switch off into a chill-out zone.

It's like a magnet, is Parknasilla. Every time you turn off down the Ring of Kerry at Kenmare, heading for Sneem or points west, with a working agenda, you can't help but feel, as you see the first signs and get near to this legendary old hotel, that, dammit, cancel work, pull up the driveway, park the car and just lose yourself for a few days. Cancel the world, we want to get off, and we want to get off at Parknasilla!

That is the effect Parknasilla engenders; it is one of the great escapes, and when you pitch up here with your family, or just for a romantic getaway, the rest of the world disappears. Sonny, Jackie, Jim and all the crew greet you like old friends, you sink into the subtle comfort, the fantastic art collection beckons you to study it closely, and the comfort food lulls you into some sort of pure joy.

And, in an age when it is fashionable to knock the workings of the State, let us note that Parknasilla is State-owned, and is a glorious success story. Long may she run.

● **OPEN:** All year
● **ROOMS:** 84 rooms
● **PRICE:** €125-€140 per person sharing. Single supplement €26. Look out for frequent offers.

● **NOTES:**
All major cards accepted. Wheelchair access.
Children welcome, beach, swimming pool, walks. Special rates available for 3-5 days' stay, full board, good value.

● **DIRECTIONS:**
15 miles from Kenmare, 3 miles from Sneem. Travel on the N70 (Ring of Kerry) and you will see their sign.

SHEEN FALLS LODGE

Adriaan Bartels
Kenmare
County Kerry
Tel: (064) 41600 Fax: 41386
info@sheenfallslodge.ie
www.sheenfallslodge.ie

The SFL is one of few places that make sense of luxury, so being here seems a necessity, and not an indulgence.

SFL manager Adriaan Bartels leads his team by example, and he leads from the front. Head chef Chris Farrell leads his kitchen team by example, and he leads from the front. The conjunction of service and food in the Sheen Falls is done by these men with true élan and understanding, and thanks to this, this distinguished hotel seamlessly goes from strength to strength, endlessly developing, always improving – new suites including a Presidential suite are just the latest addition this year alone – a crew and an hotel always striving to be better, every year.

Without this motivation to be the best – and it extends to every single element and every single member of this huge operation – SFL would be just another big pile of luxury. But the animation of the staff means that it all makes sense. It's not a high-roller indulgence. It is the application of an art form of service and creative cooking taken to a pinnacle of burnished perfection. They make sense of luxury, something few in Ireland can manage.

● **OPEN:** First Fri in Feb-2 Jan
● **ROOMS:** 66 rooms
● **PRICE:** €275-€415 per room. Supplements apply for superior rooms and suites.

● **NOTES:**
All major cards accepted. Dinner, €69. Full wheelchair access. Children welcome, 'kiddies club'. Two thatched cottages for rental, exclusively catered for.

● **DIRECTIONS:**
Heading towards Glengarriff, the hotel is on the first turn left after the suspension bridge.

SHELBURNE LODGE

Tom & Maura Foley O'Connell
Killowen
Cork Road
Kenmare
County Kerry
Tel: (064) 41013 Fax: 42135

No other house feels like
Maura Foley's glorious,
glamorous Shelburne, one
of the great destinations.

Let us praise a famous woman. Maura Foley has stepped
back from running Packie's, her legendary Kenmare
restaurant, now in the capable hands of Martin Hallissey.
For 40 years, her cooking has been a benchmark of what
Irish cooking is and can be, and she has been one of the
most significant people in Irish culinary history.

Now, with a bit more time, she will be able to concentrate fully on the glorious Shelburne Lodge, and prove
what most of us already know; that as a designer and
innkeeper, Mrs Foley is just as distinguished a practition-
er as she was a restaurateur. For Shelburne is one of the
design glories of Ireland, a house of unique temperament
and character, a house where the unwavering and precise
eye of a true artist has been brought to bear with daz-
zling efficacy. We know of nowhere else that has a feel
quite like Shelburne, and nowhere else has breakfasts so
imaginative, well-considered and well-executed, One
glory is impressive, but two glories shows true genius.

- **OPEN:** Mar-Nov
- **ROOMS:** Seven rooms, all en suite
- **PRICE:** €100-€140 per room. Single €70-€90

- **NOTES:**
No dinner (good restaurants locally). Enclosed car park-
ing. No wheelchair access.
Children welcome, high chair, cot.

- **DIRECTIONS:**
300m from Kenmare centre, across from the golf course
on the Cork road. Kenmare is 35 miles from Kerry airport, 60 miles from Cork airport.

ZUNI

**Paul & Paula Byrne, Sandra &
Alan McDonald
26 Patrick Street, Kilkenny city
Tel: (056) 772 3999
Fax: 775 6400
info@zuni.ie www.zuni.ie**

Zuni's owners exhibit the
self-criticism of the best
hoteliers, so expect this hot
address to get even better.

In design terms, Zuni isn't a perfect boutique hotel, but
it's close enough to merit a cigar and, one feels, the sis-
ters-and-husbands team who man this red-hot Kilkenny
hot spot will steadily and assuredly make it better, will
give it more of a distinct signature, as time goes by.

The template for their design progress comes from their
work in the restaurant, which was always a great room,
but which they have customised over time to make ever
better, even more welcoming and successful. Indeed,
everything about Zuni shows a consistent self-criticism
which is the hallmark of the very best hoteliers and
restaurateurs: they don't rest on their laurels.

And, while they are about the business of getting the
rooms a little less stark and a little more cosy, they should
also work on the breakfast offer, which needs to be polished. If this all sounds like a lot of criticism, we offer it
simply because Zuni has achieved so much in such a short
space of time, and because we want Zunis everywhere.

- **OPEN:** All year, except Christmas
- **ROOMS:** 13 rooms, all en suite
- **PRICE:** €45-€85 per person sharing

- **NOTES:**
Visa, Mastercard, Amex, Laser. Restaurant open for dinner Mon-Sun. Full wheelchair access. Enclosed private
parking at rear. Children welcome.

- **DIRECTIONS:**
Located in the city centre, on Patrick Street, which is
round the corner from Kilkenny Castle. Take M50 from
Dublin airport. Take N7 southbound direct to Kilkenny.

IVYLEIGH HOUSE

Dinah & Jerry Campion
Bank Place
Portlaoise, County Laois
Tel: (0502) 22081 Fax: 63343
ivyleigh@gofree.indigo.ie
www.ivyleigh.com

Dinah Campion's meticulous dedication to her calling makes Ivyleigh House one of the most immaculate, comfortable places to lay your head.

A lady from the tourist authorities once told Dinah Campion, before she opened her meticulous house to guests, that a top-flight B&B would never work in Portlaoise. Nice to get some encouragement from the voice of experience before you head into the unknown and embark on a brave new adventure.

The lady hadn't reckoned on the determined Mrs Campion. And she hadn't reckoned on the fact that when word spreads of someone who does a job as well as it can be done, that word of mouth will very soon ensure that you have a roaring success. Ivyleigh is a roaring success, because Mrs Campion does her job as well as it can be done. The extraordinary housekeeping, the intense comfort of the rooms, where every detail is chosen with such care: this is B&B keeping as an art form. Breakfast, amidst many highlights, is one of the very best. 'A fried breakfast must be cooked from the pan,' Mrs Campion asserts, and that perfectionist attention defines Ivyleigh.

● **OPEN:** All year
● **ROOMS:** Four rooms, all en suite
● **PRICE:** €55 per person sharing. Single in double/twin €75, single room €60

● **NOTES:**
No dinner. No wheelchair access. On street car parking. Children over 8 years welcome.

● **DIRECTIONS:**
Turn off M7 for Portlaoise, turn right at Church (sign for railway station) and left at next junction for 200yds and keep right at next junction. House is 30yds on right.

ROUNDWOOD HOUSE

Frank & Rosemary Kennan
Mountrath
County Laois
Tel: (0502) 32120 Fax: 32711
roundwood@eircom.net
hidden-ireland.com/roundwood

Frank and Rosemary's Roundwood House is one of the most charming, unpretentious and real of the Irish country houses: prepare to fall in love.

Abandon critical perspective, ye who enter Roundwood House. For this is not a house to be cool about, it is not a house to analyse or pontificate over. It's not a house to be indifferent about. It's simply a place to fall in love with, whatever your age, sex, nationality or shoe size. If you have any longing for romance in your soul, if you have any flibbertigibbety facility in your perspective, then you will fall under Roundwood's spell, the cynic in you will be excised, and you will quickly be enthusing to all your new best friends, as you sit and chat and drink with them around the dinner table, about what an amazing place Roundwood House is.

The cold eye which you might cast about the place, and which might remark on the ancien pauvre style and the elegantly distressed furnishings, will be dissolved in the delight of Rosemary's splendid cooking, and the irresistible bonhommie this lovely house seems to conjure from out of the ether. What an amazing enchantment!

- **OPEN:** All year, except Christmas Day
- **ROOMS:** 10 rooms, all with private bathrooms
- **PRICE:** €75 per person sharing. Single supplement €25

- **NOTES:**
Dinner, 8.30pm, €45, communal table. Book by noon.
No wheelchair access.
Children welcome, high chair, cot, babysitting.

- **DIRECTIONS:**
Turn right at T-junction in Mountrath for Ballyfin, then left onto R440. Travel for 5km on the R440 until you come to the house.

THE COURTHOUSE

Piero & Sandra Melis
Main Street
Kinlough
County Leitrim
Tel: (072) 42391
thecourthouserest@eircom.net

Piero Melis' little restaurant with rooms in pretty Kinlough is one of the key addresses in the beautiful, waiting-to-be-discovered, borderlands.

Travel the few miles from Bundoran, in County Donegal, down to Kinlough, in County Leitrim, and you move from the ridiculous to the sublime. Bundoran smells of overused cooking oil, and looks worse than it smells. Kinlough, on the other hand, is undiscovered, demure, handsome, petite, composed, a darling little space with a darling little place – The Courthouse – bidding you to stop, eat and stay the night.

The rooms are simple, as you would expect of a restaurant with rooms run by an Italian proprietor who hails from Sardinia, but the restaurant is very fine, the staff are superb, the sounds are cool, the cooking eschews any pretensions and heads straight for deliciousness. Home made raviolis are excellent, veal chops with white wine and rosemary are simple deliciousness, desserts are splendid and prices are keen. Don't miss the Sardinian wines imported by Piero, and don't miss this neat little getaway and its taste of the sublime in County Leitrim.

● **OPEN:** all year except Xmas & 2 weeks in Nov & Feb
● **ROOMS:** Four rooms
● **PRICE:** B&B €28 per person sharing, €33 single

● **NOTES:**
Visa, Master, Laser. Wheelchair access. Children welcome, but not in the restaurant after 8pm. Dinner 6.30pm-9.30pm, €30-€35

● **DIRECTIONS:**
On the main street in Kinlough, turn off the main Donegal/Sligo road at Bundoran, on the bridge opposite the post office.

HOLLYWELL COUNTRY HOUSE

Rosaleen & Tom Maher
Liberty Hill
Carrick-on-Shannon
County Leitrim
Tel & Fax: (078) 21124
hollywell@esat.biz.com

The Maher boys are making a splash with their food adventure, whilst the Maher parents continue to run a house that is a beacon of civility.

The Maher family's magical way with food and hospitality has extended its capable tentacles over the bridge and into Carrick-on-Shannon itself, as Tom and Rosaleen Maher's boys, Conor and Ronan, have been making a huge success of The Oarsman pub in the centre of the town. To see these young fellas work, to see the care they lavish on their customers and their cooking, is to see a family gene that has hospitality stamped all over it: they are peas from the pod of a family who personify all the good things of hospitality: civility, hard work, genuineness, true service, a desire to please.

And, of course, they learnt it all from their folks, who run what is simply one of the loveliest addresses in the North West. Hollywell is pretty, dignified and companionable, all because it is simply so well run by the Mahers. It's a cosy house, gaily sociable, extremely relaxing, with delicious cooking, and there is nothing about this overlooked area that the Mahers don't know. So, go exploring in Carrick.

● **OPEN:** 2 Jan-20 Dec
● **ROOMS:** Four rooms, all en suite
● **PRICE:** €46-€60 per person sharing. Single supplement €20-€30

● **NOTES:**
No dinner. Enclosed car park. No wheelchair access. Children over 12 years welcome.

● **DIRECTIONS:**
From Carrick-on-Shannon, cross the bridge, keep left at Gings pub. The entrance to Hollywell is on the left.

THE MUSTARD SEED

Daniel Mullane
Echo Lodge, Ballingarry
County Limerick
Tel: (069) 68508 Fax: 68511
mustard@indigo.ie
www.mustardseed.ie

Comfort should be Dan Mullane's middle name: no other hotelier has a style so focused on lush comfort.

Comfort should be Dan Mullane's middle name. Like some of the other design classics in this book – The Clarence, Shelburne Lodge, Glenally – Echo Lodge and its Mustard Seed restaurant is the work of a man whose skill and passion for design leads to a style which is utterly unique: no one else makes spaces like Mr Mullane, and you can't believe that anyone else could. And – his trump card – everything he does is devoted to comfort.

He could wing it on comfort alone, especially with the newer wing of suites which deserve every design prize going. But Mr Mullane congratulates his design skills with a witty hospitality that is the icing on this fabulous cake. Backed by a devoted team, Mr Mullane's hospitality animates and unifies the beautiful Echo Lodge, creating one of the most glorious destinations anywhere in Ireland. Comfort is all: comfortable rooms, comfort food, comforting hospitality, all of it quietly world-class in every way. Dan 'Comfort' Mullane. It has, well, a comforting ring to it.

● **OPEN:** All year
● **ROOMS:** 16 rooms, including three suites
● **PRICE:** €86-€140 p.p.s. Single supplement €30, triple room supplement €60

● **NOTES:**
Dinner in their restaurant, €30-€50. Give advance notice for special diets. Full wheelchair access. House not suitable for young children.

● **DIRECTIONS:**
Take the Killarney road from Adare, a quarter mile, until you reach first turning off to the left, signed for Ballingarry.

10 PLACES WITH
GREAT BREAKFASTS

1

BALLYMAKEIGH HOUSE
KILLEAGH, Co CORK

2

THE CLARENCE
DUBLIN, Co DUBLIN

3

COAST TOWNHOUSE
TRAMORE, Co WATERFORD

4

GROVE HOUSE
SCHULL, Co CORK

5

HANORA'S COTTAGE
NIRE VALLEY, Co WATERFORD

6

IVERNA COTTAGE
SPIDDAL, Co GALWAY

7

MARBLE HALL
DUBLIN, Co DUBLIN

8

NEWPORT HOUSE
NEWPORT, Co MAYO

9

SHELBURNE LODGE
KENMARE, Co KERRY

10

STELLA MARIS
BALLYCASTLE, Co MAYO

GHAN HOUSE

Paul Carroll
Carlingford
County Louth
Tel: (042) 937 3682 Fax: 937 3772
ghanhouse@eircom.net
www.ghanhouse.com

Paul Carroll covers all bases
in the charming Ghan House,
with a cookery school, special
events and a fine restaurant.

A lot of people in the hospitality business talk a great deal
about multi-functioning, about using their space for a variety of tasks and purposes. If they want guidance on the
subject, they should go and talk to Paul Carroll, at the
lovely Ghan House.

Along with rooms for residents and a fine restaurant that
also opens to non-residents for dinner at weekends, Mr
Carroll has a niche market for corporate events, runs a
small cookery school, hosts special dining events such as
his inspired Georgian nights, and all the while he acts as a
fountain of information about lovely Carlingford (you will
learn more about the town via his website than from anywhere else).

It's all mighty impressive, and it's all superbly well done, by
a man with a precise focus, indeed, a focus as precise as his
acclaimed photographer's eye. To get away to this charming town for a few days, either mid-week or weekend, and
to spend some chill-out time in Ghan is simply a delight.

● **OPEN:** All year, except 23 Dec-15 Jan
● **ROOMS:** 12 bedrooms, all en suite
● **PRICE:** €80-€90 per person sharing

● **NOTES:**
Visa, Mastercard, Laser, Amex. Restaurant open Fri-Sat,
7pm-9.30pm. Midweek & Sun by arrangement, €47. No
wheelchair access. Phone to discuss policy on children.

● **DIRECTIONS:**
Approaching from south, Ghan House is 1st driveway
on left after 30mph sign on entering Carlingford. 53
miles from Dublin, 43 miles from Belfast.

NEWPORT HOUSE

**Kieran & Thelma Thompson
Newport
County Mayo
Tel: (098) 41222 Fax: 41613
info@newporthouse.ie
www.newporthouse.ie**

Forgive the gushing purple
prose, but Newport House
is an address that unleases
the Byronic urge in us all.

Some addresses inspire you to nothing less than a tone poem to explain their attraction. Looking back on our notes about Newport House, we don't seem able to restrain the poetic flights of fancy: 'the monogrammed dressing gowns arrayed on the bed like a sleeping knight and his bride'; 'the bed turned down, the lamps lit, the blazing bedroom fire'; 'the correctness of the staff, the brilliant Catherine, the absence of television, all of it wonderfully out-of time'.

Phew! Steady on there. And that's before we get to John Gavan's cooking: 'sumptuous, rich, politely debauched, exquisite'. My goodness, we had a fine old time, didn't we? Newport weaves this sort of spell: it is an enchantment of great service, great classical cooking and a unique atmosphere. It is one of the great country houses, because it is grand, surreal, sophisticated, and quite lovely. So, apologies for the flights of fancy, but just see for yourself if you don't switch on the rapture thanks to Newport.

- **OPEN:** 19 Mar-6Oct
- **ROOMS:** 18 rooms, all en suite
- **PRICE:** Low season €104-€140, High season €115-€151. Single supplement €24, superior room supplement €22

- **NOTES:**
All major credit cards accepted.Restaurant open for casual lunch and formal dinner. Dinner €55. Limited wheelchair access. Children very welcome. Secure parking.

- **DIRECTIONS:**
In the centre of the village of Newport, on N59 route.

ROSTURK WOODS

Louisa & Alan Stoney
Mulrany, Westport
County Mayo
Tel & Fax: (098) 36264
stoney@iol.ie
www.rosturk-woods.com

Louisa Stoney is one of the most super-charged of hostesses, a woman with boundless energy and the ability to do six things at the same time.

Rosturk is a lovely house, brightly coloured, gaily decorated, tucked away in the midst of surrounding woods, and, above all, a place blessed with the flickering light that bounces off the lapping waters of Clew Bay, a light that suffuses and animates this lovely place.

Something about Rosturk seems perfectly to capture and express the wild, western-seaboard spirit of this adorable part of Mayo, on the road between Newport and Achill Island. And, if the house expresses a spirit of place, Louisa Stoney trumps it, every time, with a spirit of wilful determination. For here is one of those extraordinary women who manage to do everything, frequently at the same time, and do it charmingly and effortlessly, someone whose animation brings alive the place where they live and work. She is a true hostess: knowledgeable about the area and all its diversions, charms and specialities, a super cook should you ask her to cook dinner, and, a free spirit who makes you feel you truly are someplace special.

- **OPEN:** Mar-Nov
- **ROOMS:** Three double/twin rooms, all en suite
- **PRICE:** €45 per person sharing

- **NOTES:**
No credit cards accepted. Dinner, €30-€35. Full wheelchair access in self-catering accommodation. Secure parking. Children welcome, cot, highchair, toys.

- **DIRECTIONS:**
7 miles from Newport, heading towards Achill, after you have crossed Owengrave River, look for blue sign with Rosturk Woods. Turn left towards the sea.

STELLA MARIS

Frances Kelly & Terence McSweeney
Ballycastle
County Mayo
Tel: (096) 43322 Fax: 43965
www.StellaMarisIreland.com
info@

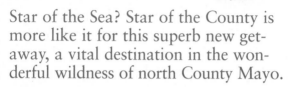

Star of the Sea? Star of the County is more like it for this superb new get-away, a vital destination in the wonderful wildness of north County Mayo.

Stella Maris is going to be one of the stars of the next decade, thanks to an irresistible location – hard by the wild waters of Ballycastle in north Mayo – and thanks to the driven and meticulous nature of Frances Kelly, a local woman who brought her spouse, Terence McSweeney, back from the 'States to undertake the task of restoring this fine old fortress-cum-convent-cum-school into a smart boutique hotel with just under a dozen bedrooms. The style of the house is understated, the hospitality is heartfelt, and the cooking – by Ms Kelly – is very fine indeed, a vibrant, unpretentious style of food that is accurately focused on the flavours of shellfish, local meats and some good sweet baking, all capably served by hip young locals who enjoy their work. For the record, our breakfast of poached plums followed by scrambled eggs, was probably the best breakfast of the year: yumola!

The splendid Ceide Fields is nearby, but that fine monument is already playing second fiddle to this new star.

- **OPEN:** Easter-mid-Oct
- **ROOMS:** 11 rooms
- **PRICE:** B&B €90-€150 per person sharing

- **NOTES:**
Visa, Mastercard, Access. Full wheelchair access.
Limited ability to accommodate young children.
Dinner 7pm-9pm (until 10pm weekends); €40

- **DIRECTIONS:**
Go down the hill from Ballycastle, and the Stella Maris is signposted from here. Turn right, it's on the Pier Road, overlooking the sea.

10 PLACES WITH
GREAT STYLE

1

BUGGY'S GLENCAIRN INN
LISMORE, Co WATERFORD

2

THE CLARENCE
DUBLIN, Co DUBLIN

3

COAST TOWNHOUSE
TRAMORE, Co WATERFORD

4

GLENALLY
YOUGHAL, Co CORK

5

ISKEROON
CAHERDANIEL, Co KERRY

6

THE MORRISON
DUBLIN, Co DUBLIN

7

THE MUSTARD SEED
BALLINGARRY, Co LIMERICK

8

QUAY HOUSE
CLIFDEN, Co GALWAY

9

SALVILLE HOUSE
ENNISCORTHY, Co WEXFORD

10

SHELBURNE LODGE
KENMARE, Co KERRY

CASTLE LESLIE

Sammy Leslie
Glaslough
County Monaghan
Tel: (047) 88109 Fax: 88256
info@castleleslie.com
www.castleleslie.com

Gothic. Gargantuan. Irresistible. Fun. Castle Leslie is a house straight out of a feverishly imagined Tim Burton movie. Except it's real, more than real.

Actually, let's be honest: even Tim Burton would be hard pressed to conceptualise something as out-of-the-ordinary as Castle Leslie, a place where everything is other worldly. The utterly insouciant scale and the gloriously cheeky chutzpah of this monument to human indulgence are unparalleled in Ireland, which perhaps explains why people love it so much. If you want to feel like you are on a movie set – Mr Burton is ready for your cameo, madam – then Castle Leslie is the place to be: simply turning up at CL makes you feel different, so different.

It also makes you act different, as Sammy Leslie wends you into her calm hospitality, and Noel McMeel's superb cooking puts the cherry on the icing of this loveable folly. It is the kind of place where guests quickly become friends, touring the rooms together, winding the night away with drinks in front of the fire. If you can only see the somewhat faded splendour – as we did for too long – then you are missing the point, so simply surrender.

● **OPEN:** all year, including Christmas
● **ROOMS:** 14 rooms
● **PRICE:** B&B €125-€225 per person sharing

● **NOTES:**
Visa, Mastercard. No wheelchair access.
No children under 18 years.
Dinner 6pm-9.30pm, €55

● **DIRECTIONS:**
2 hours from Dublin off the N2. Just under 2 hours from Belfast. Detailed directions can be e-mailed or faxed.

HILTON PARK

Johnny & Lucy Madden
Clones
County Monaghan
Tel: (047) 56007 Fax: 56033
mail@hiltonpark.ie
www.hiltonpark.ie

Hilton Park offers one of the truly great country house experiences, an occasion that can be described as sublime.

Every so often, an e-mail will land on our computer, sent by Johnny Madden. Now, when many people in the world of hospitality contact you, it is usually to tell you something about themselves and their place. But, with Mr Madden, the e-mails are always about things going on in his neck of the woods, new projects by new people in the zone that he wants to bring to our attention.

And, what's more, he never, ever writes about Hilton Park, or what he and Lucy Madden are getting up to with their glorious, gargantuan house and gardens. Too modest, too discreet. And, what's more, he never tells the folk he writes about that he is spreading the good news of their work. Too modest, too discreet.

This sort of selfless behaviour is typical of the man, and it's the sort of good grace that makes Hilton one of the very finest of Irish country houses. Yes, it's expensive to stay here and to eat this great cooking, but it is an experience that is truly unique: there is nowhere else like it,

- ● **OPEN:** Apr-Sep and year round for block bookings
- ● **ROOMS:** Six rooms, all en suite
- ● **PRICE:** €110-€150 per person sharing, B&B

● **NOTES:**
Visa, Mastercard. Dinner, 8pm (8.30pm Fridays), €47.50, book ahead. No wheelchair access. Secure parking. Not suitable for children under 8 years.

● **DIRECTIONS:**
77 miles from Dublin. Take N3 to Cavan, Cavan by-pass, leave at 2nd junction, go through Ballyhaise and Scotshouse and Hilton is next entry on left, after golf club.

CROMLEACH LODGE

Christy & Moira Tighe
Castlebaldwin, via Boyle
County Sligo
Tel: (071) 9165155, Fax: 9165455
info@cromleach.com
www.cromleach.com

We reckon that if Cromleach Lodge
set out to be a little more relaxed and
laid-back, it might just discover a
whole new, interesting lease of life.

Cromleach Lodge is one of those addresses which tends
to make us think beyond the critical remit. Yes, we admire
the big bedrooms, and we enjoy Moira Tighe's precise
and polished cooking.

But on a quiet evening, when there is little atmophere in
the place and when the service seems stilted, we wonder
what Cromleach would be like if its prices were pitched
to local pockets rather than the deep pockets of high-
roller tourists. We wonder would the food speak more of
itself if these perfect ingredients were not so polished
and primped, if the food simply didn't try so hard. And we
wonder what it would feel like if the staff — literally and
metaphorically — let their hair down, unbuttoned those
jackets, stopped behaving as if they were in an hotel in
Zurich. We have a notion that Cromleach might be the
better for all this, that it might seem more welcoming,
less frosty, if it was happy to be itself, rather than trying
to be a bit posh. It's a lovely place. It just needs to relax.

● **OPEN:** Feb-Nov
● **ROOMS:** 10 rooms, all en suite
● **PRICE:** B&B €120-€188 per person sharing. Single
supplement €45

● **NOTES:**
All major cards accepted. Dinner €55. Wheelchair
access with assistance. Children welcome, high chair, cot,
babysitting. Private family room.

● **DIRECTIONS:**
Signposted from Castlebaldwin on the N4. 3 hours from
Shannon airport, Dublin and Belfast.

TEMPLE HOUSE

Deb & Sandy Perceval
Ballymote
County Sligo
Tel: (071) 83329, Fax: 83808
guest@templehouse.ie
www.templehouse.ie

You meet the most fascinating, enlivening people at Temple House, every single time you stay here.

icon

You always meet such interesting people at Temple House. It doesn't matter what time of year you visit – high season, or winter time for some field sport getaway time – for whenever you pitch up the mighty, winding drive and walk in, the folk who are your fellow guests are always mighty attractive, interesting guys and girls.

How do Sandy and Deb Perceval manage this? Do they have some manner of screening that eliminates anyone who is not individually fascinating? Or is it just that the word-of-mouth about Temple attracts people who are zany, left-field, curious and charming? We don't know. What we do know is that Temple House is a peerless country house, and a peerless experience that is always slightly magical, summoning all the best that is in us, elevating us and civilising us, and giving something to the optimist and the epicurean that resides in all our hearts.
Important Note: Host is very allergic to scented products. Ask for details before booking.

- **OPEN:** 1 Apr-30 Nov
- **ROOMS:** Six rooms
- **PRICE:** €60-€65 per person sharing. Single supplement €20. Single room €65

- **NOTES:**
Visa, Mastercard, Amex accepted. Dinner, 7.30pm, €30. High tea for children under seven, 6.30pm.
No wheelchair access. Private parking. Children welcome, rocking horse.

- **DIRECTIONS:**
Signposted off the N17 10km south of the N4 junction.

INCH HOUSE

John & Nora Egan
Thurles
County Tipperary
Tel: (0504) 51261/51348
Fax: 51754 inchhse@iol.ie
www.inch/house.com

A charming, comfortable country house with comfort food and genuine hospitality, the Egan family's Inch House is a key Midlands address.

Look closely back over your head when you walk into your room in John and Nora Egan's Inch House. Above the door, there will be a small figure of Christ on the cross. It is a typically devout and modest gesture from these devout and modest people, the Egans, and it is surely the signature of their sweet, comfortable house; someone to watch over me.

Any grandeur that Inch enjoys – and in an understated way it enjoys a lot, especially the stained glass window and the beautiful William Morris room, which is a real gem – is tempered by the quiet, hard-working nature of the Egans. Kieran O'Dwyer's satisfying, winter country cooking fits like a hand into a glove in this context, and you crave and get some creamy potato gratin with roast lamb, and buttery sweet profiteroles for pudding. It's a place to loosen the belt and relax, which makes it a key address for travellers but also for locals who value this demure destination address. Charming and genuine.

- ● **OPEN:** All year, except Christmas
- ● **ROOMS:** Five rooms, all en suite
- ● **PRICE:** €52.50 per person sharing, Single €60

● **NOTES:**
Dinner 7pm-9.30pm Tue-Sat, €40. No wheelchair access. Children welcome, cot, high chair, babysitting on request.

● **DIRECTIONS:**
Four miles from Thurles on the Nenagh road. Turn off at the Turnpike on the main N8 road, signpost Thurles.

LEGENDS TOWNHOUSE

Michael & Rosemary O'Neill
The Kiln, Cashel
County Tipperary
Tel: (062) 61292
info@legendsguesthouse.com
www.legendsguesthouse.com

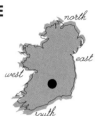

Michael and Rosemary O'Neill are professionals to their fingertips, and the spectacular location of their house – right beside the Rock! – is fantastic.

You have always wanted to stay in a house that was right smack at the foot of the Rock of Cashel, haven't you? You have. So thank heavens for the lovely Legends, for that is right where it is smack at the foot of the Rock. Michael & Rosemary O'Neill's pretty house has the most staggering location: as you eat dinner in their excellent restaurant, the Rock towers and lowers just outside the window, awesome and inspiring, and only a few steps away.

The location – the house is also just a stone's throw off the main N8 Dublin-Cork road – is spectacular, but the hospitality of the O'Neills, and especially Mr O'Neill's measured, delicious and impressive cooking, really places extra cherries on the icing on your cake. It is this combination of effects, underscored by some truly professional service, that makes the whole Legends' experience so fine. If you want delicious, signature cooking, a cosy room and a night away from the kids, then it's ace. If you are touring in search of your ancestors, then it's incredible.

● **OPEN:** All year, except two weeks in Nov & Feb
● **ROOMS:** Seven rooms, all en suite
● **PRICE:** €64 per person sharing

● **NOTES:**
Restaurant open for dinner Mon-Sun, €43-€45. No wheelchair access. Children - family rooms, but no children under 10 years in restaurant.

● **DIRECTIONS:**
From the N8, take the R660 to Holy Cross, Legends Restaurant and Townhouse is the fourth house on the left hand side.

AN BOHREEN

Jim & Ann Mulligan
Killineen West, Dungarvan
County Waterford
Tel: (051) 291010
mulligans@anbohreen.com
www.anbohreen.com

Ann Mulligan's heavenly cooking, and fantastic value for money make An Bohreen a one-of-a-kind place that should be on everyone's N25 route.

An Bohreen is a one-of-a kind place you can't afford not to go to, for the standard of cooking from Ann Mulligan and the amazing value for money make for one hell of a combination.

You might not think this at first, when you turn off the N25 at the top of the hill and drive the short distance to this relatively modest bungalow. But the detail of the interiors – geo-thermal heating, for instance, and a grand sitting room and dining area – shows the professional acumen of the Mulligans. And then the cooking! Mushrooms stuffed with cheese and crab. Celeriac soup with Cashel Blue croutons. Marinated pork loin with sautéed York cabbage. West Waterford lamb with jus lié and garlic. Heavenly baking such as chocolate mocha tarte with fresh cream and a blackcurrant sauce. And if you go off to bed singing, breakfast is worthy of a choirful noise: hot baked scones with whiskey marmalade; cheese blintz with apple sauce; ginger crêpes with sautéed apples. Fab.

- **OPEN:** Mar 17-end Oct
- **ROOMS:** Four rooms
- **PRICE:** €34-€36 per person sharing. Single rate €47-€49

- **NOTES:**
Visa, Mastercard, Amex. Dinner 7pm, €32, book by noon. No wheelchair access. Secure parking.

- **DIRECTIONS:**
From the N25, after the town of Lemybrien, look for the resume speed sign. 3.1 miles later there is a right turn, travel 200yds and you will see a sign for the house.

ANNESTOWN HOUSE

John & Pippa Galloway
Annestown
County Waterford
Tel: (051) 396160 Fax: 396474
relax@annestown.com
www.annestown.com

An undiscovered location of stunning natural beauty and the comfort of Annestown House: that will do us very nicely indeed, thanks very much.

The Copper Coast, as the strip of coastline between Dungarvan and Tramore in County Waterford is known, is one of the most elemental, beautiful, and undiscovered parts of Ireland. How it has remained so undetected is something for which we should all give grateful thanks, especially as other areas around the coastline have been ravaged by low-quality tourism development.

And, perhaps the nicest way to give thanks, is to pay the Copper Coast the compliment of a visit, in which case you will have the added joy of encountering another elemental, understated little gem, John and Pippa Galloway's Annestown House, hard on the hill in the village. The Galloways are pioneering people: they opened Annestown as a dedicated restaurant - probably the first in Waterford - way back in 1977, and their considerable professional experience gives Annestown its just-right air of quiet confidence, making it the golden nugget in the Copper Coast, the perfect place to stay way down south.

- **OPEN:** mid Mar-end Oct
- **ROOMS:** Five rooms, all double or twin
- **PRICE:** B&B €50-€70 per person sharing

- **NOTES:**
Amex, Visa, Mastercard accepted. Dinner, €35, 7.45pm Mon-Sat, book by previous bedtime. No wheelchair access. Partially enclosed parking. Children welcome.

- **DIRECTIONS:**
6 miles west of Tramore on R675. 12 miles from Waterford, 16 miles from Dungarvan. Signpost from Tramore.

BUGGY'S GLENCAIRN INN

Ken & Cathleen Buggy
Glencairn, nr Lismore
County Waterford
Tel & Fax: (058) 56232
buggysglencairninn@eircom.net
www.buggys.net

Ken and Cathleen Buggy's unique Glencairn Inn is the most mesmerising, magical address in the country.

icon

'To Buggy's in Glencairn. First time for us. Loved it. Despite reading several times that there is in fact no village of Glencairn, still surprised at this lovely guesthouse at the side of the road. Room was full of character and tons of books, mirrors and drawings. Really comfortable. Had a bottle of Sancerre sitting outside in the sunshine... relaxing is not the word.'

This note from a friend is typical of the sort of reaction first-time visitors have to Ken and Cathleen Buggy's heavenly restaurant, bar and rooms. There really is nowhere that compares to Buggy's. Everything here, from the style to the cooking to the animated nature of Ken himself, is in a class of its own, in a box of its own. 'The most inspiring place. That man is so special', was how a well-known food writer described Mr Buggy after a working visit. Mr Buggy is simply that rarest of animals; an original, and he brings his originality to his cooking, his design, his unique way of thinking. So treat yourself to some true originality.

- ● **OPEN:** Jan-end Nov
- ● **ROOMS:** Five rooms, all en suite
- ● **PRICE:** B&B €110-€120 per room, €70-90 single

- ● **NOTES:**
Dinner from 7.30pm-9pm, booking essential, €35. Secure car parking. No wheelchair access. No facilities for very young children.

- ● **DIRECTIONS:**
In Lismore turn right at the monument, go to Horneybrook's garage, there is a sign to Glencairn. Follow this road for 3 miles, until you come to the Inn.

AN CARN

Deuglán & Siobhán O'Reagain
Ring, Dungarvan
County Waterford
Tel: (058) 46611 Fax: 46614
ancarn@eircom.net
www.ancarn.com

Bilingual menus in Irish and English signal your arrival in the Gaeltacht area of West Waterford, and An Carn accentuates that acute sense of place.

You get a real sense of place when staying in Deuglán and Siobhan O'Reagain's An Carn, sited as it is in the West Waterford Gaeltacht.

The menus are bilingual, and the food brings that sense of place as close to home as it can get, for their food is sourced from local folk: Tony Dunphy's T-bone steak, made hip thanks to a balsamic jus; Helvick salmon with a good crab and chardonnay sauce; Tounafulla black pudding with smoked Gubbeen cheese; down to the waters at Helvick again for some crab claws, these sweet morsels warmed in garlic butter; their own version of the classic banoffi which is done in An Carn as a banoffi mousse pie, further proof of just what a talented sweet baker Mrs O'Reagain is. Lovely ingredients, lovely cooking, and we reckon the best way to enjoy it all is to book one of the simple rooms that they offer, make a night of it, enjoy the extraordinary views, and let that West Waterford Gaeltacht air seep into your soul.

● **OPEN:** All year (weekends only Sept-Easter)
● **ROOMS:** Four rooms
● **PRICE:** €40 per person sharing. Single €45

● **NOTES:**
Visa, Mastercard, Laser. Dinner 6.30pm-9.30pm Tue-Sat, 12.30pm-2pm Sun lunch.
Full wheelchair access.
Children welcome.

● **DIRECTIONS:**
Turn off N25 for Ring and follow signposts. 1km up the hill from Mooney's Pub.

COAST TOWNHOUSE

Turlough McNamara & Jenny McNally
Upper Branch Road
Tramore, County Waterford
Tel: (051) 393646 Fax: 393647
coastrestaurant@eircom.net
www.coast.ie

Having made Coast restaurant a sure-fire hit, McNamara & McNally are set to make Coast Townhouse the hit of 2004.

Turlough McNamara enjoyed a steep learning curve when working with Hugh O'Regan and John Rocha on the opening of The Morrison Hotel, in Dublin, and he is bringing all the acute expertise learnt there, along with a stylish personal savvy, to bear on the quartet of rooms that comprise Coast Townhouse.

With glass-cased bathrooms that boast the most gorgeous Italian fittings, luxurious colours, a bricolage of furniture, neat sound systems with personalised CDs and a range of smart accessories, Coast is going to be the bling-bling destination of 2004, just as Coast restaurant has been the bling-bling restaurant destination of 2003. McNamara and his partner, Jenny McNally, are truly hip, authoritative guys, people who set the zeitgeist that the rest of the hospitality world chases after. Well, everyone in hospitality is going to be making their way down to Tramore, along with all the style magazine editors, so you had better book early to get a taste of the new thing.

- **OPEN:** All year
- **ROOMS:** Four rooms
- **PRICE:** €50-€75 per person sharing

- **NOTES:**
Visa, Mastercard, Amex, Laser. Dinner served 6.30pm-10.30pm Tue-Sun, 1pm-3pm Sun, Dinner €40. No wheelchair access.

- **DIRECTIONS:**
Take the R673 from Waterford city. Just up from the beach front road in Tramore, the entrance is on Upper Branch Road. Look for the signs.

GORTNADIHA

Eileen & Tom Harty
Ring, Dungarvan
County Waterford
Tel: (058) 46142
ringcheese@eircom.net
waterfordfarms.com/gortnadiha

Eileen Harty's lovely B&B, set high
and handsome on the hill of Ring, is
an archetypal bed and breakfast, with
great comfort and great cooking.

Having been one of the gathering of Irish artisan farmhouse cheesemakers, proud maker of Ring cheese, Eileen
Harty has re-invented herself as an outstanding B&B
keeper, in charge of a great, hospitable house.

There is no mystery as to how she should have been able
to switch careers so seamlessly: she is a sociable woman,
a great hostess, and her métier is sharing: sharing her
lovely house, sharing her food, right down to sharing
information about excellent new places to stay that she
has encountered, places that sing with the tenor of high
standards that drive women such as Mrs Harty to do
their very best.

And high standards are what Gortnadiha House is all
about. It's a high, handsome farmhouse on the hill as you
ascend towards the summit of Ring, and the rooms are
calm and comfortable, the breakfast a veritable panjan-
drum of choice things. And Mrs Harty's sociable nature
brings the whole charming escapade all together. Super.

- **OPEN:** 1 Feb-1 Dec
- **ROOMS:** Three rooms, all en suite
- **PRICE:** €30-€40 per person sharing

- **NOTES:**
No dinner. No wheelchair access. Children welcome.
Visa, Mastercard accepted. Private parking.

- **DIRECTIONS:**
Follow the curve of Dungarvan Bay. Come off the N25
at the junction for Ring (3km west of Dungarvan).
Signposted from here. Midway between Waterford and
Cork. 2 hours from Rosslare.

HANORA'S COTTAGE

Seamus & Mary Wall
Nire Valley, nr Clonmel
County Waterford
Tel: (052) 36134 Fax: 36540
hanorascottage@eircom.net
www.hanorascottage.com

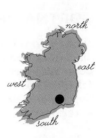

The first time you
encounter the Hanora's
breakfast is one of the
great travel experiences.

They are the true West Waterford pioneers, the Wall
family. Now that this glorious region has become quietly
renowned for great food, and for great hospitality, we
should remember that Seamus and Mary Wall were here
long before anyone else, establishing the sort of standards
in Hanora's Cottage which others, who have come along
later, have had to emulate in order to become successful.
Blessed be those who create the template, for that is
what the Wall family have done with their food, their hospitality, their joie de vivre. West Waterford needs them.
The part of the template which no others can emulate is,
of course, their staggeringly brilliant breakfasts, a feast
which is surely the best in the country. The first time you
encounter the Hanora's breakfast is one of the great
experiences of travelling in Ireland. It is just the tonic to
get you out walking in the hills of the beautiful Nire Valley,
with the promise of Eoin Wall's cooking in the restaurant
just the thing to bring the day to a blissful, happy end.

- ● **OPEN:** All year, except Christmas
- ● **ROOMS:** 10 rooms
- ● **PRICE:** €75-€85 per person sharing. Single occupan-
cy of double room €80-€100. Room 5, €125

- ● **NOTES:**
Restaurant open 6.30pm-9pm, €40. Wheelchair access.
No children. Secure parking.

- ● **DIRECTIONS:**
From Clonmel or Dungarvan, follow signs to
Ballymacarbry village. The house is signposted from
there.

POWERSFIELD HOUSE

Eunice Power & Edmund Power
Ballinamuck West, Dungarvan
County Waterford
Tel: (058) 45594 Fax: 45550
powersfieldhouse@cablesurf.com
www.powersfield.com

Eunice and Edmund Power's pretty house boasts some of the finest cooking you can enjoy in West Waterford, and that is really saying something.

Is it God who is in the detail, or the Devil? The answer is, if you get the detail wrong, it's the Devil. But if you get it right, then it's God, for sure.

So, in Eunice Power's lovely Powersfield House, you can rub feng shui shoulders with the Almighty, for Mrs Power's attention to detail is only mighty. She has an acute eye for colour which makes her bedrooms fresh, light and appealing. She has an eye for texture, which makes the design of the dining room and the little lounge area comfortable and welcoming. And she has the ability to put the right object in the right place, so the house feels grand, even though it is actually rather modest.

All of these virtues sing out, above all, from Mrs Power's cooking. Breakfasts are a true treat, and amongst the most imaginative you can enjoy. Dinner in the dining room showcases some terrific cooking, with great country flavours and vivid creativity. This is a fab escape in beautiful West Waterford, and splendid value for money.

- **OPEN:** All year, except Christmas and New Year
- **ROOMS:** Six rooms, all en suite
- **PRICE:** €45-€55 per person sharing. Single room €55-€65

- **NOTES:**
Amex, Visa, Mastercard, Laser. Dinner for guests only, €33.
Full wheelchair access. Children welcome.

- **DIRECTIONS:**
Follow Clonmel road from Dungarvan, the house is the second turn to the left, and the first house on the right.

RICHMOND HOUSE

Paul & Claire Deevy
Cappoquin
County Waterford
Tel: (058) 54278, Fax: 54988
info@richmondhouse.net
www.richmondhouse.net

Richmond House is one of
the very best places to eat
and stay, with a charming
naturalness all its own.

Paul and Claire Deevy's Richmond House is one of those
rare addresses that just gets better and better. The
Deevys were fairly young when they assumed control of
Mr Deevy's family home, and every year since they have
grown more confident, more capable, more capacious in
their ability to deliver exactly what people want.

What's to love? The lot. The cooking, for starters, is some
of the very best country house cooking you can eat in
Ireland, and Paul Deevy and his assistant, Maria Wall, have
been fizzing with culinary magic for some years now. The
service, under Claire Deevy, is as good as it gets: here is
a woman in complete control of the dining room, assist-
ed by charming local ladies who bless this pretty house
with an unfusssy naturalness.

And the rooms are splendid, and offer splendid value for
money, which means that Richmond has the lot. But, make
sure to book in advance, for the word is spreading fast
about the stellar charm of this key Waterford address.

- **OPEN:** 20 Jan-20 Dec
- **ROOMS:** Nine rooms
- **PRICE:** from €65 per person sharing, Single supple-
ment €20

- **NOTES:**
Restaurant open for dinner only, Mon-Sun (closed on
Sun in winter), €45. No wheelchair access.
Private parking. Children welcome, babysitting, cots,
toys.

- **DIRECTIONS:**
Just outside Cappoquin, the house is well signposted.

TEMPLE COUNTRY HOUSE & HEALTH SPA

Declan & Bernadette Fagan
Horseleap, Moate
County Westmeath
Tel: (0506) 35118 Fax: 35008
info@templespa.ie
www.templespa.ie

If the body is a temple, then your temple needs to be introduced to the ultimate temple for the body, Declan and Bernadette's brilliant Temple Spa.

A spa is a place where there is a curative mineral spring, says the dictionary. Well, we don't believe that Declan and Bernadette Fagan's fabulous house actually has a curative mineral spring, but what we do know for certain is that Temple is an unparalleled fount of curative goodness. Nowhere else takes you out of yourself and into a parallel world of bliss the way Temple does. And this curative power is not just thanks to the I-so-need-this treatments which the Temple therapists offer for guests, though those treatments are sublime and reviving. Instead, the curative powers extend right down to the cooking and hospitality of the Fagans themselves. Mrs Fagan has a profound gift for looking after people, for understanding what they need even before they recognise it themselves. Her cooking, then, is a vital part of the whole concept of Temple as a spa: this is food to recharge your batteries and your soul, great cooking that is light, energising, fantastically flavoursome. You deserve Temple Spa, you do.

- **OPEN:** All year, except Christmas
- **ROOMS:** Eight rooms, all en suite
- **PRICE:** €225 p.p.s. for 24 hours midweek, Single €245. €395 p.p.s. Fri-Sun, €435 single. Three days midweek from €555 p.p.s., €605 single. All inclusive rates only.

- **NOTES:**
Mastercard, Visa, Amex accepted. Dinner, 8pm. Inclusive rates only. No wheelchair access. Children over 16 years.

- **DIRECTIONS:**
Half a mile off the N6 Dublin-Galway road, and clearly signposted just after Horseleap, heading westwards.

WINEPORT LODGE

Jane English & Ray Byrne
Glassan, Athlone
County Westmeath
Tel: (090) 643 9010, Fax: 648 5471
lodge@wineport.ie
www.wineport.ie

Wineport Lodge has already entered the national psyche as one of the great escapes and hideaways for stressed city folk, so head for the lake!

Like any great success story, Wineport Lodge seems always to have been with us. This beacon of great hospitality and great design in the Midlands has already become such a home-from-home for those stressed by city life, that it's hard to imagine it has only been around for not a lot more than a year.

The rooms in the Lodge are amongst the best designed and best decorated you can stay in, with views out across the lough that are captivating in their simple elementalism: sitting here, gazing out across the water, the city isn't an hour away, it's a lifetime away.

Ray Byrne and Jane English have always been the most perspicacious and capable owners, navigating this busy restaurant and rooms into national recognition. They call it a wine hotel, but the theme is confined to naming the rooms and the residents' lounge, and is never overstated. Wineport is a great escape, and breakfast on the verandah of your room, gazing out over the lake, is divine.

- **OPEN:** All year
- **ROOMS:** 10 rooms
- **PRICE:** €220-€275 double room rate, Single occupancy, Sun-Thu €175, Fri-Sat €220-€275

- **NOTES:**
All major cards accepted. Restaurant serves dinner, à la carte menu approx €55. Full wheelchair access.

- **DIRECTIONS:**
At Athlone, take the Longford exit off Dublin/Galway rd, fork left at the Dog & Duck, Lodge is 1 mile further on on the left.

10 PLACES NEAR MAJOR
ROADS, PORTS & AIRPORTS

1
BALLYMAKEIGH HOUSE
N25

2
CARRIG HOUSE
THE RING OF KERRY

3
COAST TOWNHOUSE
WATERFORD AIRPORT

4
LEGENDS TOWNHOUSE
N7/N8

5
MERRION HALL
DUN LAOGHAIRE PORT

6
THE MUSTARD SEED
SHANNON AIRPORT

7
THE OLDE POST INN
N3

8
RED BANK LODGE
DUBLIN AIRPORT

9
STELLA MARRIS
KNOCK AIRPORT

10
WINEPORT LODGE
N6

KELLY'S RESORT HOTEL

Bill Kelly
Rosslare
County Wexford
Tel: (053) 32114 Fax: 32222
kellyhot@iol.ie
www.kellys.ie

The eye-poppingly gorgeous
Beaches dining room is the
latest part of Kelly's Hotel
to be glorified by fab design. *icon*

How do they do it, tell us that? Everyone who stays at
Kelly's reckons that it can't be improved. How can you
improve someplace that is pretty darn perfect?

But Bill Kelly and his team don't think like that. And so,
every year, they use their wintertime break to make some
part of the hotel better than it was. You thought the dining room sublime, one of the finest in the country? Just
go and see it now – it's been renamed 'Beaches' – and see
how rigorous self-questioning and striving for absolute
perfection can allow these guys to take something perfect
and make it even better. Beaches is a glory.

And, as such, it is simply the latest glory in Kelly's, for their
bistro, La Marine, is a glory. The wine list is a glory. The art
collection is a glory. The food is a glory. The service is a
glory. And the staff are a glory unto themselves, a benchmark team whose civility is unmatched. And so, every
year we return and we are surprised – delightfully surprised – by the ever-greater glory of Kelly's Resort Hotel.

- **OPEN:** Late Feb-early Dec
- **ROOMS:** 99 rooms, all en suite
- **PRICE:** Spring/autumn: weekend rate €285 p.p. + 10%
service charge; 5-day midweek rate €550 p.p. + 10%
service charge. Summer: 7day rate €880 p.p. + 10%

- **NOTES:**
All rates include full board. La Marine restaurant also
comes recommended. Full wheelchair access. Every facility for babies and children.

- **DIRECTIONS:**
Clearly signposted in Rosslare and from the main road.

McMENAMIN'S TOWNHOUSE

Seamus & Kay McMenamin
3 Auburn Terrace
Redmond Road, Wexford
County Wexford
Tel: (053) 46442 mcmem@indigo.ie
www.wexford-bedandbreakfast.com

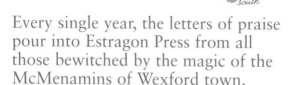

Every single year, the letters of praise pour into Estragon Press from all those bewitched by the magic of the McMenamins of Wexford town.

Every year they flood in, the letters of tribute to the hospitality skills of Seamus and Kay McMenamin. From Bangor, they praise 'the standard of the cooking... meant that we had an outstanding breakfast every morning' From Dublin, they write in praise of this 'particular gem... to say that their breakfasts set a benchmark is an understatement – they were superb'. From Brecon, they praise, in particular, the breads baked by Kay, 'an object lesson in how to elevate the staff of life to celebrity status. Wonderful'.

For these acolytes – hell, for these groupies – McMenamin's is quite simply the place, the only place, to stay in Wexford. 'We invariably use the fare as a yardstick to judge other offerings on our side of the Irish Sea', they write from Wales, concluding, 'Haven't found an equal yet!'. 'We haven't had as good in any hotel or guest house anywhere in Ireland', the Bangorians write of the cooking. High praise, and the McMenamins are worth it.

- **OPEN:** All year, except Christmas
- **ROOMS:** Five rooms, all en suite
- **PRICE:** €45 per person sharing. Single €50

- **NOTES:**
No dinner. No wheelchair access.
Locked parking. Children welcome, high chair, cot, babysitting.

- **DIRECTIONS:**
In the centre of Wexford, directly opposite the bus and railway stations. Beside the large Dunnes Stores supermarket.

SALVILLE HOUSE

Jane & Gordon Parker
Salville, Enniscorthy
County Wexford
Tel: (054) 35252, Fax 35252
info@salvillehouse.com
www.salvillehouse.com

Salville is one of the most individual and sublime of Irish country houses, an oasis of calm, and ace food.

What we love about Salville House is the quiet under-statement of everything that makes this great escape tick. The subtlety of the design, the confident style, the mellow furnishings, the way in which this house is allowed to be itself, the way it is allowed to have a character that speaks of its history and its owners, the meticulous and capable Jane and Gordon Parker.

You cannot be as good as this couple are at their job – and they are amongst the very best hosts and cooks – without having a very clear idea of exactly what you want to achieve, and exactly how you want to do it. Put this understatement and this driven vision together, and you get something special indeed, a place where every detail is crafted with the precision of artists at work. Mr Parker's cooking has won enormous critical acclaim, and it is worthy of every piece of praise. Not only is it superb country cooking, executed to a standard other country houses could only dream of, it is superb value for money.

● **OPEN:** All year, except Christmas
● **ROOMS:** Five rooms. One two-bedroom self-contained apartment available for B&B or self catering
● **PRICE:** €50 per person sharing

● **NOTES:**
Dinner, 8pm, €30. No wheelchair access. Secure parking. Children welcome.

● **DIRECTIONS:**
Leaving Enniscorthy on the N11 to Wexford - take the first left after the hospital, go up the hill to a T-junction then turn left and proceed for half km.

BALLYKNOCKEN HOUSE

Catherine Fulvio
Glenealy, Ashford
County Wicklow
Tel: (0404) 44627 Fax: 44696
cfulvio@ballyknocken.com
www.ballyknocken.com

The cooking in lovely
Ballyknocken is amongst
the best Irish country cooking you can find, and enjoy.

Catherine Fulvio's cooking in the lovely, pert, petite Ballyknocken House is sublimely delicious, thanks to the cook's skills, and to the most careful sourcing of her ingredients. One of Mrs Fulvio's allies, for instance, is Synott's butchers in Rathdrum, and we can tell you that after we stayed here, and after we had enjoyed a superlative dinner and a superlative breakfast, we drove from Ballyknocken to Rathdrum, found the inauspicious Synott's brothers shop, and brought home some of the very best beef we have eaten in recent years.

Mrs Fulvio also sources from the local farmers' markets, and her meticulous nature has made her into an expert on Wicklow's food sources. She brings all these good things home, then, and cooks some of the most delicious country cooking that you will find anywhere in Ireland: above all, do not miss the meat cookery. Put this great food together with a most pretty house and the fulsome hospitality of Catherine, and you have a dream getaway.

- **OPEN:** Feb-Nov
- **ROOMS:** Seven rooms
- **PRICE:** From €49.50-€59 per person sharing. Single supplement €28

- **NOTES:**
Visa, Mastercard. Dinner, Mon-Sat, €34. No wheelchair access. Children welcome. Cookery school opens Feb.

- **DIRECTIONS:**
From Dublin, head south to Ashford (on N11), then turn right after Chester Beatty pub. Continue for 3 miles and the house is on the right.

THE BROOK LODGE INN

Evan, Eoin & Bernard Doyle
Macreddin Village, Aughrim
County Wicklow
Tel: (0402) 36444 Fax: 36580
brooklodge@macreddin.ie
www.brooklodge.com

Evan Doyle's Brook Lodge Inn is not just a country hotel and restaurant: it is the fulcrum of the community, and a beacon of super-high standards.

Its early success has been so great that Evan Doyle's Brook Lodge Inn is already set to grow and expand, adding further rooms and facilities. Such success is a tribute to the holistic vision and holistic conception which Mr Doyle created here, out of a green field site.

For the Brook Lodge is not merely a fine restaurant with comfortable rooms. It is also home to a farmers' market, a venue for good music, as romantic a place to get married and have a wedding reception as you will find, and it is precisely the bringing together of all these complementary things that makes this inspiring place work. The Brook Lodge, in other words, is part and parcel of the community, and not simply a destination for stressed Dubliners to crash out.

What's to love? We love the public rooms – such a successful melding of Ballymaloe and Assolas – and the super-romantic Strawberry Tree restaurant, and the great service by switched-on staff. A pioneering destination.

● **OPEN:** All year, including Christmas
● **ROOMS:** 55 rooms and suites
● **PRICE:** €87.50-€135 per person sharing, single supplements apply. Check web for rates for B&B and Dinner.

● **NOTES:**
All major cards accepted. Restaurant, pubs, market and bakery, dinner €48. Secure car parking. Reservations essential. No wheelchair access. Children welcome.

● **DIRECTIONS:**
N11 to Rathnew. Right at r'about, to Glenealy, on to Rathdrum. 1 mile outside Rathdrum, right towards Aughrim.

NORTHERN IRELAND

ANNA'S HOUSE

Anna Johnson
Tullynagee, 35 Lisbarnett Rd
Comber, County Down
Tel: (028) 9754 1566
anna@annashouse.com
www.annashouse.com

Anna's is an enchanting house and garden, and it's a cult favourite with food lovers thanks to organic-only produce for dinner and breakfast.

Anna cooks, Ken pours the wine and chats and bakes the breads, and you haven't been in Anna's but five minutes and there you are sitting in the kitchen with a sloe gin in your hand and you feel as if you have known this pair all your life. There is a powerful instinct for hospitality enshrined by this couple that overwhelms everyone, and this gorgeous house and gardens, and Anna's superb cooking, using only organic foods, weaves a spell around the visitor. Organic vegetables have come no further than the garden, and their bounteous flavours showcase the work of a cook with true culinary intelligence. If dinner is a delight, breakfast – with your culinary senses triggered by the smell of fresh-baked breads – is a joy: dill and parsley omelette, homemade jams and Seville orange marmalade, fresh espresso, sweet-stewed damsons, and fresh scones straight from the oven. Time, then, to stroll around the garden and bask in its secret garden air of mystery. 14 miles from Belfast: a million miles from the modern world.

● **OPEN:** All year, except Christmas
● **ROOMS:** 3 rooms
● **PRICE:** stg£30 per person, stg£35 single

● **NOTES:**
Dinner by request. Secure car parking.
No wheelchair access. Babies in arms welcome, but not suitable for children.

● **DIRECTIONS:**
In Lisbane pass the petrol station, turn right into Lisbarnett Road. After 0.6 miles & after a right hand bend follow a private concrete lane leading up the hill.

ASH ROWAN

Evelyn & Sam Hazlett
12 Windsor Avenue
Belfast, County Antrim
Tel: (028) 9066 1758
Fax: 9066 3227
ashrowan@hotmail.com

The evergreen Ash Rowan sails sublimely onwards, delighting the regulars who turn up here time and again
for Sam and Evelyn's hospitality.

'We take great care about our breakfast and we want you
to write about it!' So say Sam and Evelyn Hazlett, the
alpha and omega of lovely Ash Rowan, but the remark is
all too modest. For breakfast in Ash Rowan offers everything, from the most superlative Ulster Fry, that glorious
concoction that pays proper tribute to the pig and which
is served with both soda farls and potato bread in the
North. Before that, there is tipsy porridge – a shot of
Drambuie and cream to act as a hair of the dog - and
there are Edwardian breakfast staples such as kedgeree,
and fresh fish of the day, pan-fried in herb flavoured butter. But, don't forget the house special of mushrooms
flambéed in sherry with cream, or the Irish Scramble
which mixes three (3!) eggs with bacon, mushrooms and
a little grated cheese. Vegetarians are well looked after,
and Continentals can get a Continental breakfast, if they
are crazy enough. It's bounteous, brilliant, and typical of
the generosity that beats at the heart of Ash Rowan.

- **OPEN:** All year, except Christmas
- **ROOMS:** Six rooms, all en suite
- **PRICE:** from stg£79-£96 per person sharing, stg£48
single

- **NOTES:**
Dinner 7pm, stg£28, separate tables. Reservation essential, 24 hours' notice required. Locked car parking. No
wheelchair access. Children over 12 years welcome.

- **DIRECTIONS:**
Windsor Avenue is the 3rd Avenue on the right, off
University Road, past the Botanic Inn.

BEECH HILL COUNTRY HOUSE

Victoria Brann
23 Ballymoney Road
Craigantlet, County Down
Tel: (028) 9042 5892
info@beech-hill.net
www.beech-hill.net

Victoria Brann's elegant and gracious house shows all the hallmarks of a true, motivated professional.

Beech Hill has a handsome architectural timelessness about it. You would hardly believe, looking at this confident, one-and-a-half storey house, set amidst rich agricultural land, that it was already more than 40 years old, for it looks so contemporary, so modern, so unusual for Northern Ireland, where suburbia and Victorianism tend to do battle, with little else in terms of design.

Victoria Brann has the right sort of confident stylist's eye to suit the house, and the interiors are decorated just right: restrained, colourful, concordant, everything summoning up a deeply relaxing comfort, especially the capacious public rooms. Ms Brann is an exacting hostess, someone in whom 25 years of working as a Cordon Bleu-trained chef shows in every detail of her work in the house, and yet she throws off all her hard work with a shrug, as if it was little or nothing. But the secret of Beech Hill is the exacting standards and hard work of the hostess, and it's a treat to enjoy the work of one so capable.

- **OPEN:** All year
- **ROOMS:** Three rooms
- **PRICE:** stg£64 for double room, £45 single

- **NOTES:**
Mastercard, Visa. No dinner. Wheelchair access with assistance. Secure parking. Children over 12 years only.

- **DIRECTIONS:**
15 minutes from Belfast city airport. Leave Belfast on the A2. Bypass Holywood. 1.5 miles from bridge at Ulster Folk Museum, turn right Ballymoney road, signed to Craigantlet. House is 1.75 miles on left.

THE MOAT INN

Robert & Rachel Thompson
12 Donegore Hill
Templepatrick
County Antrim
Tel: (028) 9443 3659 Fax: 9443 3726
themoatinn@talk21.com

The Moat Inn is Northern
Ireland's benchmark
address: nobody does it half
so well as Robert & Rachel.

'It's where you'd spend every high day and holiday', exult-
ed our editor after a recent night spent at the lovely
Moat Inn, Robert and Rachel Thompson's fab house.
Why so? 'Exquisitely comfortable and fascinating... oozes
character, charm and quirkiness'. Hmm, good start, but
wait: there's more. What did we think about Rachel's
cooking? 'Imaginative, lively, homely food which uses lots
of delicious cheeses, fruits, nuts spices and herbs': onion
tart with honey and orange dressing; roasted Cashel Blue
pears with toasted hazelnut salad; courgette and almond
soup; loin of pork with sweet thyme sauce; char-grilled
sea bass with ginger dressing and toasted sesame; crème
brûlée with griddled bananas; chocolate fudge tart with
cream. Now tell me your mouth's not watering! It is, it is.
And, in conclusion? 'With such special places to stay in
Ireland, who needs holidays abroad?' Indeed.
*Note: Robert and Rachel are moving to a grand new address
early in 2004 (see below). Follow that couple!*

- ● **OPEN:** Open all year
- ● **ROOMS:** Three rooms, all en suite
- ● **PRICE:** B&B stg£35 per person

● **NOTES:**
New address from early 2004 will be: Marlagh Lodge,
Moorfields Rd, Ballymena. Same telephone number and
fax. Visa, Mastercard, Switch. Dinner 8pm (book by noon)
stg£25. No wheelchair access. Children welcome.

● **DIRECTIONS:**
At Templepatrick roundabout roundabout, follow brown
signs to Donegore.

A

Aberdeen Lodge **56**
Aherne's **29**
Allo's Townhouse **76**
An Bohreen **106**
An Carn **109**
Anna's House **124**
Annestown **107**
Annestown House **107**
Aran Islands **71**
Ardara **52**
Ash Rowan **125**
Ashford **121**
Assolas Country House **30**
Athlone **116**
Aughrim **122**

B

Bagenalstown **21**
Ballingarry **93**
Ballsbridge **56**
Ballycastle **98**
Ballyknocken House **121**
Ballylickey **46**
Ballyliffin **55**
Ballymakeigh House **32**
Ballymaloe House **31**
Ballymote **103**
Ballynahinch Castle **63**
Ballyvolane **33**
Baltimore **47**
Bantry **46**
Barnabrow **34**

Barrowville Townhouse **20**
Beech Hill Country House **126**
Belfast **125**
Blacklion **23**
Blair's Cove House **35**
Blindgate House **36**
Bow Hall **37**
Brook Lodge Inn, The **122**
Browne's **57**
Buggy's **108**
Butlerstown **44**

C

Caherdaniel **82**
Cappoquin **114**
Captain's House, The **77**
Carlingford **95**
Carlow **20**
Carrick-on-Shannon **92**
Carrig House **78**
Cashel **105**
Castle Leslie **100**
Castle Murray House Hotel **49**
Castlelyons **33**
Castletownshend **37**
Clarence, The **58**
Clifden **66, 73, 75**
Clifden House **25**
Clones **102**
Cloverhill **24**
Cloyne **34**
Coast Townhouse **110**
Comber **124**

Connemara **63-64, 66-67, 69, 73-75**
Cork **39**
Corofin **25-26**
Costello **67**
Courthouse, The **91**
Courtmacsherry **48**
Coxtown Manor **50**
Craigantlet **126**
Croaghross **51**
Cromleach **102**

D

Delphi Lodge **64**
Devon Dell **65**
Dingle **77, 80**
Dolphin Beach **66**
Dublin **56-62**
Dunfanaghy **54**
Dungarvan **106, 109, 111, 113**
Dunkineely **49**
Durrus **35**

E

Emlagh House **80**
Enniscorthy **120**

F

Fergus View **26**
Fermoyle Lodge **67**

Fortview House **38**

G

Galway **65, 68, 72**
Galway Harbour Hotel **68**
Garnish House **39**
Garraunbaun House **69**
Ghan House **95**
Glaslough **100**
Glenally House **40**
Goleen **38**
Gortnadiha **111**
Green Gate, The **52**
Grove House **42**

H

Hanora's Cottage **112**
Hawthorn House **81**
Hilton Park **101**
Hollywell Country House **92**

I

Inch House **104**
Inishowen **55**
Iskeroon **82**
Iverna Cottage **70**
Ivyleigh House **89**

INDEX

K

Kanturk 30
Kelly's Resort Hotel 118
Kenmare 81, 84, 86, 87
Kilgraney Country
    House 21
Kilkenny 88
Killarney 83
Killarney Park Hotel,
    The 83
Killeagh 32
Killorglin 78
Kilmurvey House 71
Kilnaboy 26
Kinlough 91
Kinsale 36

L

Laghey 50
Lahinch 27
Leenane 64
Legends Townhouse 105
Leighlinbridge 22
Letterfrack 74
Letterkenny 51
Lismore 108
Listowel 76
Longueville House 43
Lord Bagenal Inn 22

M

Macnean Townhouse 23

Mallow 43
Marble Hall 59
McMenamin's Townhouse
    119
Merrion Hall 60
Mill, The 54
Moat Inn, The 127
Moate 115
Morrison, The 61
Mountrath 90
Moy House 27
Moyard 69
Mustard Seed, The 93

N

Newport 96
Newport House 96
Nire Valley 112
Norman Villa 72

O

Olde Post Inn, The 24
Otto's Creative
    Catering 44

P

Park Hotel, The 84
Parknasilla 85

Portlaoise **89**
Portsalon **51**
Powersfield House **113**

Q

Quay House, The **73**

R

Recess **63**
Red Bank Lodge, The **62**
Renvyle **74**
Richmond House **114**
Rock Cottage **45**
Rossaor House **55**
Rosslare **118**
Rosturk Woods **97**
Roundwood House **90**

S

Salthill **72**
Salville House **120**
Schull **42, 45**
Sea View House
    Hotel **46**
Sea Mist House **75**
Shanagarry **31**
Sheen Falls Lodge **86**
Shelburne Lodge **87**
Skerries **62**

Slip Way, The **47**
Sneem **85**
Spiddal **70**
Stella Maris **98**

T

Temple Country House &
Health Spa **115**
Temple House **103**
Templepatrick **127**
Thurles **104**
Tramore **110**
Travara Lodge **48**

W

Westport **97**
Wexford **119**
Wineport Lodge **116**

Y

Youghal **29, 40**

Z

Zuni **88**

'For the native it might be a shock to discover the riches that abound here. For the visitor, for whom there is no other way to discover the best places to eat and shop for food, the Bridgestone Food Lover's Guide to Northern Ireland is, quite simply, indispensable.'

**SETH LINDER
THE IRISH NEWS**

'An invaluable gourmet reference for both round-the-country ramblings and sourcing the best grub in your home town... packed with great information on local markets, producers and pubs with grub.'

**LOUISE EAST
THE IRISH TIMES**

The companion volume to this guide is...

The Bridgestone
100 BEST RESTAURANTS IN IRELAND 2004

'Ireland is lucky to have a reliable restaurant guide - something Britain has never achieved. The Bridgestone 100 Best Restaurants in Ireland, *by John and Sally McKenna combines sound taste and essential information.'*

Paul Levy, The Wall Street Journal